Not Your Average Joe

Profiles of Military Core Values and Why They Matter in the Private Sector

★ ★ ★

By Dennis Davis

Copyright © 2013 Dennis Davis
All rights reserved.

ISBN: 1480143987
ISBN 13: 9781480143982

Library of Congress Control Number: 2012919939
CreateSpace Independent Publishing Platform,
North Charleston, SC

Not Your Average Joe:
Profiles of Military Core Values and Why they Matter in the Private Sector

★

Praise for *Not Your Average Joe*

"Public opinion polls rank the military near the top of the list of most admired professions - above clergy, teachers, business executives and even, surprise, elected officials. This is largely due to the high ethical standards demanded of our military members at all levels. Lapses that might be tolerated or overlooked in other professions will end a military officer's career. 'Duty, Honor, Country' isn't just a good quote: it is a way of life for our Soldiers, Sailors, Airmen, and Marines. Dennis has written an important book that should be required reading for every person who wants to understand why the people in uniform deserve such respect."

Brigadier General Dennis W. Schulstad, USAF, Retired

★

"*Not Your Average Joe* is not your average book. Dennis has crafted a wonderful resource for employers to use in understanding the exceptional core values that veterans bring with them when they transition into the business world. This is a must-have resource for all hiring managers and HR departments."

Lieutenant Colonel Alex Plechash, USMC, Retired
U. S. Naval Academy Class of '75

"Today's veterans are a breed unto themselves and are certain to surpass the 'The Greatest Generation' in their willingness to sacrifice their lives for our country. Unlike those before them, these fine young Americans willingly volunteer to answer their countries call in a time of war. For without them, then who? Who would willingly stand up to fight for this great country?

These Soldiers, Airmen, Sailors and Marines are highly trained and educated, capable of making insightful and precise decisions that are uncommon among most of today's youth. They offer a level of passion, commitment and integrity that are common place in today's military and sought after by employers who previously stood in their boots.

In my 26 years of service, I was continually amazed at their resilience, commitment and willingness to achieve any goal set before them. They truly are a profession of arms and capable of so much more than some give them credit for. I've seen them in combat, during emergency relief efforts and peace time and they always rise to the occasion regardless of the situation. They have an irreplaceable ability to solve problems, manage time, or develop better and more efficient means of addressing issues.

Dennis captures this very spirit and essence of a generation of Americans who have demonstrated a commitment to a higher calling. He offers a unique insight into their devotion to higher values, morals and ethics. He also captures their distinct skills and ability that categorize them in a class above those who have not served in the same capacity. A must read for business and industry leaders."

Command Sergeant Major Edward "Scott" Mills,
MN ARNG, Retired

To my girls - Joy, Gabrielle, Caroline, and Annaliese.

You are my inspiration to pursue my dreams. Without your support
my dreams would not be possible. I am proud of each of you.
Never stop chasing your dreams!
All my love.

To Colonel John N. Worley, USAF, Retired
Leader, loyal follower, faithful husband, father, friend.
My time with you was short; your impact on my life was large.
We miss you and love you. Keep watch over us in the wild blue yonder.

Table of Contents

Foreword by Minnesota State Senator Ted Daley ix

Introduction xiii

Chapter 1: The True Test of Honor – The Licorice Test 1

Chapter 2: Kenny Rogers's *The Gambler* Equals Integrity? 17

Chapter 3: Selfless Service – There Is No "I" in Team 29

Chapter 4: Excel - Not Just a Spreadsheet but Also a Core Value? 41

Chapter 5: Integrity – The Common Thread Woven into the
          Core Values Tapestry 53

Chapter 6: The Journey from Selfish to Selfless Service 65

Chapter 7: Programming Your Moral Code - Integrity 75

Chapter 8: Strength – The Bond That Holds a Team Together 85

Chapter 9: Integrity – Black and White or Fifty Shades of Gray? 95

Chapter 10: Why Hire Joe? Values Versus Skills Based Hiring 107

Honoring Those Who Have Served 113

Thank You To Our Sponsorship Partners 116

Foreword

DUTY

During the past two years, it has been my distinct privilege to lead the Minnesota Senate on veterans' issues, both for the opportunities it has provided to build relationships with members on both sides of the aisle, and more important, for the profound honor to recognize our veterans and their families for everything they have given our nation.

When a Senator resides in a "safe" senate district, the path to reelection can be fairly smooth, depending on the composition of the district (whether it is predominantly conservative or liberal). Conversely, a tough district comprises many independent-minded voters who may swing their vote from one party to the other nearly every election cycle; they often represent the key votes to a small margin of victory in every election. Controversial issues and votes during the recent legislative session, a Senator's likability, and a Senator's constituent service often determine whether the incumbent is able to secure another term in office.

As I live in a swing district, a number of "friends" have asked me to "take a walk" on particularly difficult issues to avoid upsetting people on either side. Some people consider this to be an advantageous move as a short-term political tactic. However, over the course of my life, whether at home, as a student at West Point, or in the Army, I have learned the right course is not to avoid the tough decision or to take the easy way out. Rather it is my *duty* to face these challenges directly. When I was sworn into office, I took an oath to uphold and defend the Constitution. The oath did not specify this action in regard to only the easy votes but in regard to *all* decisions. Duty calls us to take the harder path, to choose the road less traveled, and to face our fears directly. Knowing I must do my duty, when those calls to "walk" on an issue arise, I already know what the answer will be. I will be there. I must be there. It is my duty, and I always will answer the call to stand and not simply walk away.

HONOR

The history of the Honor Code at West Point dates back to its inception in 1802 when the Honor Code within the officer corps meant simply that an officer's word was his bond; this remains true today. "A cadet will not lie, cheat, or steal, nor tolerate those who do." Those thirteen words are the honor code by which all West Point cadets live while attending the US Military Academy in New York. I was a student there during the 1980s while President Reagan served as our Commander in Chief. It amazed my friends back home in Minnesota that I could leave a five or ten dollar bill and a handful of change on my desk, and two weeks later every single nickel would be right where I had left it.

West Point graduates are frequently referred to as members of the Long Gray Line, due to the color of the uniforms its cadets wear. As I recall those cadet days, I see that the institution and its leaders were very similar to my parents in their approach to honor, honesty, and integrity. There wasn't a moral relativity but always a certainty about the clear distinction between right and wrong. Though we were part of the Long Gray Line, there was very little gray in the area of honor and integrity; that part of our lives was black and white.

At West Point I witnessed honor in action, where two or three cadets shared barracks rooms; rooms were always unlocked and nothing ever was stolen. For me honor is a nonnegotiable commodity; integrity is something we earn through years of toil and is certainly not something to barter, negotiate, or give away. The best example I've ever heard of integrity in action is "Doing the right thing when no one is looking."

COUNTRY

Selfless sacrifice is deeply ingrained in the mindset of every Soldier; it begins at basic training and continues throughout their careers. Every service member makes a transition from a self-centered life to one focused on the needs of others. The rifleman next to me in Baqubah, Iraq, put his life on the line for me. He did so not for fame, glory, or stock options but because he and the others in the squad served with honor, and their core values required them to be willing to pay the ultimate sacrifice for me and any other member of the unit. I was fully prepared to do the same for them.

The call to serve this nation as a member of the military is not one our youth take lightly these days, knowing they are likely to serve in harm's way. Our young servicemen and women are courageous, loyal, and respectful. Since 9/11, I've served with them in Israel, Cuba, England, Iraq, and across the United States. They deeply desire to be a part of something bigger than themselves. Serving in our armed forces in the twenty-first century, they have earned this privilege. As the world's lone superpower, the United States has a global responsibility. In accepting these duties, our service members take on a remarkable number of responsibilities across the globe.

Today's troopers are definitely not your average Joes. They understand cutting-edge technology better than ever before, use it on a daily basis, and have built a work ethic that is typically stronger than that of their Generation Y peers. Whether they complete their service obligation or remain active in the Reserve component, these world travelers have seen and experienced twenty-first century commerce like nothing their fathers or grandfathers ever witnessed. To their core their values are "Duty, Honor, and Country." Are these values you could use in your company? If so, consider hiring more veterans. I am proud to serve my country in the military and my state in elected office. More than that I am honored to help define the value of the veteran in employment beyond military service and humbled to be a part of this project to clearly show why we are anything but your average Joes.

Ted Daley
Minnesota Senator, Senate District 38, 2010–2012
West Point, Class of '88
Lieutenant Colonel, US Army Reserve

PS_BX02310975

createspace

CreateSpace
7290 Investment Drive Suite B
North Charleston, SC 29418

Question About Your Order?

Log in to your account at www.createspace.com and "Contact Support."

06/04/2013 11:10:52 AM
Order ID: 42544661

Qty.	Item
	IN THIS SHIPMENT
1	Not Your Average Joe 1480143987

Introduction

"Joe" is one of many terms used to refer to someone serving in the military. Those outside the military may be more familiar with hearing the phrase "G.I. Joe" used to describe someone who is serving. It seems even from the youngest ages everyone knows who GI Joe is, almost as if we are born with an understanding of who is in the military but without understanding what they really do. Years ago I remember stopping at a friend's house to drop something off and happened to do so in uniform. One of her young children came to the door before she could answer and peeked out to see who was visiting. Excitedly he ran as fast as his little feet could take him to announce that G.I. Joe was at the front door!

Often the understanding of "Joes" ends with simply the knowledge that they serve and little more beyond that. Without a clear understanding or reference point as to what military personnel do or who they are, people often fill in the details using whatever information they have, such as the latest news story or Hollywood movie. Unfortunately this rarely creates an accurate picture of military service and the value "Joes" could bring to employment beyond the military. Stereotypes portray veterans as, among other things, steely-eyed killers who show up at 0500 hours every morning and demand that everyone in the office does PT. Those in the office might not even know what PT (physical training) is, but they are afraid of it and certain it will involve many painful variations of a pushup. The stereotypes continue; people often believe vets constantly bark orders, are not being team players, are inflexible, and have no ability to think on their own; if they are not barking orders, they are waiting to be told what to do. They believe vets call everyone "sir" or "ma'am," but these people often ignore the respect that comes with being called "sir" or "ma'am." They perceive vets as people who love war and live for the kill; as a result, they believe all vets suffer from post-traumatic stress disorder (PTSD). Unfortunately this often leaves veterans on the outside looking in when being considered for employment, especially when they make their initial transition out of the military. Without assistance in translating their value and an internal structure that understands the value "Joes" bring, the number of canned e-mail responses veterans receive that politely decline them for further consideration quickly grows.

As is often the case, there is a grain of truth to many of the stereotypes that exist. However, there is a much larger disparity between the stereotype and reality. It is this disparity I seek to explore. In this book I clearly define why "Joes" are anything but average as well as the value "Joes" bring that is directly transferable to employment in the private sector. Core values are a belief system instilled in military personnel, and they live out these values each day they serve, regardless of military status. Most companies also clearly define their core values and go so far as to display them on their websites for the entire world to see. Of course many organizations assume their work is done merely because they have held seemingly endless committee meetings and rolled their values out to employees on fancy brochures and posters to hang around the office. After all, their core values have been made public for the entire world to see; therefore they are automatically internalized and lived out daily. But are they really? A look at the number of major corporate scandals over the last twenty years suggests otherwise.

The military does many things right, but perhaps one of the things they do best, which leads to success in many other areas, is building and internalizing core values from day one in those who serve. These values drive everything "Joes" do. If they have a question regarding whether they should proceed with a specific course of action, it inevitably comes down to how they have been trained and what their core values would have them do. The military translates values such as integrity, courage, excellence, leadership, and vision beyond mere words on a website to characteristics that guide everything they do. Ask a recently separated veteran what the core values are for the branch of service they were in, and they are likely to repeat them to you verbatim while explaining in greater detail what each one means to them. Often those who served decades ago also can readily recall these values and tell many personal stories of how they lived those values over the years since they separated.

In this book I profile a group of veterans, some who served many years ago and others who still serve today. All have attained various levels of success in the military and possess skills that are directly transferable to life outside the service. You will read their amazing stories and real-life examples of how they have internalized core values and lived them out daily. In short you will see why they are not your average Joe. Indeed they are *so* much more.

Dennis Davis
www.metafrazo.net/partners.htm
www.linkedin.com/in/dennisdavis

"Every good citizen makes his country's honor his own, and cherishes it not only as precious but as sacred. He is willing to risk his life in its defense and its conscious that he gains protection while he gives it."

- Andrew Jackson

Chapter 1
The True Test of Honor - The Licorice Test

The US military is one of the most diverse work environments in the world. People from every corner of the country, and the world, voluntarily raise their hands to serve. It is a rather unique environment where members bring their unique heritage to become part of a small and exclusive team that requires the utmost discipline and trust in those with whom they serve. Rene Montero is just one example of thousands who typify this phenomenon. A native of Puerto Rico, he found his way through military service to a permanent home in Minnesota and now serves in the Minnesota Army National Guard.

Rene's father served in the Army, and in part, the transition into the military was a natural fit for him. His story of why he enlisted is a familiar one to most. He knew he wanted to serve; he wasn't ready for college; and he wanted to find a way to leave home. The military provided a vehicle to accomplish all three goals. While it was a natural fit for him, if you met Rene today while at your local coffee shop grabbing your daily mocha or latte, there is little aside from the haircut that would lead you to believe that he serves in the military. He is quiet, polite, unassuming, and small in stature. Certainly he does not match the stereotypical picture of the G.I. Joe action figure many paint in their minds when imagining a warrior.

Not Your Average Joe

Rene began his military service in 1986. He entered on a delayed enlistment while still in high school and began his service right after graduation. He has been to more schools than most, and after twenty-six years in the military, he still relishes nearly any opportunity to learn something new. To say he has a passion for learning would be an understatement. He grew up speaking Spanish, so that has come naturally for him; English is actually his second language. Since entering the service, Rene has become a fluent Spanish speaker in ten different dialects while obtaining proficiency in multiple languages, including German, Croatian, Arabic, some Russian, and others. He is a veteran of eight combat deployments and fourteen non-combat deployments. He has traveled the world, serving in Central and South America, Europe, Africa, and at the South Pole. He also served in the Persian Gulf during Desert Storm and more recently Operation IRAQI FREEDOM, where he served directly in Iraq.

Rene never lacks for a yarn to spin into an exciting story about his experiences in the Army. While he has the ability to spin the yarn, as is the case with many veterans, he is selective about whom he lets into those parts of his life. That said, if he makes a connection with you, it is one of quality and typically for life, lest you do something egregious that would betray his trust in you. He is fiercely loyal and tends to surround himself with likeminded people. When one merely views his external demeanor, it is easy to form a very inaccurate picture of who he really is. Lifting back the well-weathered curtain reveals so much more. He is a loving husband and father who is dedicated to serving others in many ways. He is a man of strong faith, which has played a key role in the development of his character both in and out of the military.

Given Rene's experiences during his twenty-six years in the service, it would be easy to understand if he had difficulty choosing the one thing that has meant the most to him. In typical Rene fashion, however, he has no difficulty clearly defining who he is and what has meant the most to him over the years. He has lived his life and built a career around one very simple concept: "Am I making a difference? If not, why and what can I do to change this?" He is not simply a policy director seeking to manage his impact from a desk; rather he prefers hands-on situations where he can impart the

THE TRUE TEST OF HONOR - THE LICORICE TEST

knowledge he has collected during his years of service, knowledge that can benefit one and all. Rene is a big-picture thinker; when training others he focuses on making the greatest impact through working to improve attitudes, which can be extremely challenging. As an expert on preparing others for combat, Rene is keenly aware that attitude is everything when completing missions safely and efficiently. Listening to Rene speak about his training methods easily could leave an impression that he is a callous and hard-nose man who cares little about his students and enjoys leading them on the most difficult paths possible. Nothing could be further from the truth. While his standards are high and he will not compromise them in any way, training others has become his life's work. Few know more about the situations one will face on a combat deployment, and Rene's job is to prepare his students to go to war and, more important, give them the necessary survival skills to make it through the deployment as safely as possible, preferably alive. Through the comprehensive training he has provided over the years, many owe him a debt of gratitude for helping them do the best job they could and giving them the ability to make it home safely. Over the years, numerous students have returned to thank him for the skills he taught them and to tell him how these skills kept them alive in dangerous situations. Without question, Rene has made a tremendous difference in the thousands of lives he has touched in his training.

If Rene were to list all of his accomplishments, it would be a very long list; he truly has been there and done that when it comes to military service. When asked, "What is your greatest accomplishment?" he gives a humble answer. He still enjoys serving and is proud that he has stuck it out to make a career of it. More important, he has received tremendous value from all of his training and has received ample opportunities to share this value with others. His biggest accomplishment, as he sees it, is the value he has brought to others during his years of training thousands of students. He not only has trained those serving in the US military but also other military personnel from around the world; most of the time he executed his training not in English but in the students' native tongue, all the while taking time to ensure that what he did fit within their cultural customs. This humility is typical Rene; he finds his greatest value not in what he has done on his own but rather in what he has given others to assist them in their own success. Several times foreign militaries have asked for him by name for assistance with their training, and numerous times he has been honored with foreign awards rarely bestowed upon outsiders.

Rene's most meaningful value is honor; this came up time and again in our conversations. His other core values are woven throughout what he defines as honor. Not surprisingly, when the conversation turns to his biggest disappointments, he says they revolve around this value, or lack thereof. Rene's word is his bond; nothing more is needed, and he always will deliver. Honor has shaped him throughout his service while he deployed in support of both Gulf Wars. He doesn't start a job he isn't prepared to finish, but he's also been disappointed by certain policy decisions, which, in his opinion, left the job undone and required US troops to go back for a second time. He also felt promises were made to the people of Iraq that were not upheld, making our task the second time around infinitely more difficult.

Having seen many areas of Iraq, he is respectful of the history in the region and its role as the cradle of civilization, one that dates back thousands of years. With so much history there, he is disappointed many more cannot see it for themselves, including his own family. Over the years he has witnessed many policy changes, some good, others not so much. He expresses disappointment in leaders who allow policy changes to be enacted without considering the impact their decisions will have, especially those that appear to abandon promises made to others and leave the US with less honor. He does not direct this disappointment at any one person or administration; many bear the responsibility of such poor decisions, he says. It is this intrinsic motivation to serve honorably that drives Rene's decision-making process, one that tries to take into account the impact of a decision not only on himself but also on his team and others involved. He has grown throughout his career while learning just as much from those who make poor decisions as those who have developed the ability to make the right decision at precisely the right time.

Rene has few personal disappointments, and only one did he feel worthy of sharing with me. Early on in his career, he was training in one of the most

THE TRUE TEST OF HONOR - THE LICORICE TEST

difficult schools the Army had to offer. It was extremely demanding physically and mentally, but he made it through until the last week of the course. It was a school where even if you completed it you still had to be invited to stay and become a part of the team. He did everything right physically and academically but wasn't asked to stay as a team member. The decision didn't devastate him, but it was discouraging. In the end the decision wasn't based solely on his physical attributes but also on his maturity. He was young, and they felt he wasn't ready to take on a higher level of responsibility. Rene came to terms with this many years ago, but his disappointment lies not with his failure to make the team but rather his decision not to return to the school when he had grown older and possessed the maturity they were seeking. While disappointed personally, he sees great value and honor in the decision leadership at the school made not to pass him on to the next round of training. He checked all the boxes and should have moved forward, but he wasn't a fit; the leadership knew it, and looking back on it, he knows it too. It is this philosophy that is woven into the fabric of his decision-making abilities; just because one can do something does not mean they *should* do something. It has to *fit,* and if it doesn't, in his line of work it could get people killed; this is an unacceptable risk to take simply because someone checked all the boxes and was "due." No one is due, ever.

Rene is one of the most resilient people I know. Through church and other activities, I've had the privilege of getting to know him on a personal level, so he shares more with me than he may share with others. We share some similarities in our journey as well, which has led to a deeper friendship. As is true for many veterans, unless you have traveled the same or a similar road as they have, it is unlikely they will share their journey with you. When our discussion turned to how Rene felt he has incorporated his core value of honor during his service, his story becomes deeply emotional and is clearly something that has and will continue to affect him for the rest of his life. Rene has deployed numerous times around the world. Part of the benefit of serving in the Reserve Component (the Guard or Reserve) is the bonds that are built with those with whom you serve over many years. Although active duty members rotate duty stations every couple of years, the Reserve Component does not, and often people can spend their entire careers based in one location. This builds strong teams and a camaraderie that is second to none. Rene was with a group of soldiers in Iraq with whom he had deployed just a couple years earlier to Kosovo in 2004; he shared a familiarity with them that only comes from time spent together over years of service. For Rene this bond included missing the birth of one of his three children and sharing the news with his team while they were thousands of miles away from home. They were a band of brothers and supported one another through both the happy times and the desolate spaces where their journey took them.

This particular deployment to Iraq was a journey through many desolate spaces. What had begun as yearlong deployment in support of Operation IRAQI FREEDOM grew into a twenty-two month activation with several unexpected extensions of service, which gave the 1st Combat Team, 34th Infantry Division the distinction of serving on the longest continuous single-unit combat operation deployment during Operation IRAQI FREEDOM. The unexpected delays in redeployment placed enormous stress on family members who were anxiously awaiting word of when they would be reunited with their loved ones; the delays also took a heavy toll on the deployed and made it difficult to keep morale high. It wasn't just the stress of not knowing when one's mission would come to an end but dealing with all of it in a combat environment that felt endless. This combat environment had life-changing consequences for Rene and his entire unit.

Rene has seen his share of difficult times, and through it all, he has overcome tremendous obstacles. His time in Iraq provided multiple obstacles that tested his limits, the weight of which would have almost certainly overwhelmed those who have never worn the uniform and faced such difficult times. In early January 2007, one such obstacle arose. As a senior noncommissioned officer, Rene trained and mentored many of the junior personnel as well as officers. A seasoned combat veteran, he had insight many did not; it is this insight that makes him a valued mentor. On January 9th, members of his unit were on foot patrol in Fallujah. They had trained for this extensively and were far enough into the deployment to have experienced many patrols without incident. No training could have prepared them for what was to come. As is often the case, an IED (improvised explosive device) exploded

The True Test of Honor - The Licorice Test

without warning, unleashing its deadly force on everyone in the kill zone. The team comprised many individuals he had mentored, several with whom he had previously deployed, and one with whom he had spent extensive time training in a collateral duty they both shared. Several members were hit, one mortally wounded; it was the same soldier Rene had mentored and with whom he had taken a special interest both personally and professionally. A mentor and mentee share a special bond that is deepened by life experiences; years earlier on the deployment to Kosovo, one of Rene's children was born on this same day, January 9th. What should be one of the happiest days of the year for Rene is now forever associated with deep loss and sorrow.

Rene is a selfless individual who sacrifices all for the good of the team and the mission at hand. As with many who share this quality, he sometimes takes on more than he needs to. Throughout his training and leadership development, he has learned that he has broad shoulders, and they are big enough to carry the burdens of his team so that they are free to face their mission with a laser focus and dedication to a successful outcome. This works well until the weight of the burdens become more than any one person can or should bear. In the aftermath of the loss of January 9th, Rene's shoulders were indeed broad, but he might not readily admit how close he has come to collapsing under the weight of the burdens he has carried.

Rene was not on the mission that day, and when they suffered a casualty, someone he had personally trained and certified as more than capable of handling any challenges in his way, survivor's guilt quickly set in. Immediately he questioned what he could have done to better prepare for *that* mission on *that* day. Was there a tool he could have given or knowledge he could have imparted that would have affected the outcome? By comparison, Rene was a seasoned veteran and his brother-in-arms was young and had his whole life ahead of him. Why couldn't Rene have been there? Could he have intervened in the situation to change the outcome? Should he have been there and taken the impact of the blast so that his mentee might have lived? One of many challenges surrounding this loss for Rene is that there are no real answers to these questions, because every answer raises several more questions that cannot be answered.

Perhaps the most difficult challenge after a casualty is lost is that everyone involved still has a mission to do. They cannot lose sight of the reason they are there, and regardless of the loss, they must press forward. Numerous times Rene has borne the brunt of these burdens, taking on tasks so his unit could take a moment to mourn the loss before moving to the next mission. Another incident previous to this one occurred months earlier and resulted in a loss of life. The vehicles from this mission came back to the base with gear that needed to be accounted for. Rene did what no human should ever have to do; he cleaned and accounted for the items that were contaminated with the aftermath of the explosion and the subsequent casualty. Those sights, sounds, and smells are forever seared into his mind and never will completely go away. Rene honored his troops that day and has continued to honor the memory of his fallen brother-in-arms. As with any loss, there is a fine balance between honoring someone's memory and holding so tightly to his or her memory that it throws off the balance in other areas of life.

Five years later, Rene continues to work through the process of honoring those who lost their lives in the line of duty yet releasing himself of the burden he has carried since those fateful days in Iraq. I have seen tremendous growth in Rene in the time I have known him, and he slowly forges ahead down the road of recovery and release. During Memorial Day weekend 2012, we held a special service at our church that honored those who have served, and Rene participated with an eager yet somewhat reluctant enthusiasm. I saw Rene do two very important things that day. First he remained true to his values and honored the memory of not only the ones he had lost but also all who have served and those who have sacrificed so much for our freedom. Second, and perhaps more important, he shared his burden with us. This was a huge step forward for him and a powerful reminder for all who attended. Although Rene has broad shoulders and can bear almost any burden, the congregation collectively has even broader shoulders and willingly stepped in to help him carry his burden and lighten his load. For any leader, military or otherwise, lessons in humility and letting go can be difficult to learn.

A separate and equally painful incident happened just prior to Christmas in December 2006. Again it was an IED that shattered the monotony of the mission that day, killing two and critically injuring a third. As was the case with the January 9, 2007 incident, Rene had a close and personal relationship with one of the soldiers who was hit. Unlike the previous incident, this soldier did not die but was critically wounded; he lost both of his legs, and the rest of his body suffered significant trauma. While death is always hard to deal with, in some ways it can be less difficult to adjust to life without a friend, as it is final and can't be changed. In the case of a traumatic injury, nothing is final; in fact life is constantly changing. The grief and anxiety felt after the initial event can be relived over and over again with every status update, every surgery, and every recovery period. Family dynamics change, as does your relationship with the family, but to what end? Numerous questions about the future quickly arise, while answers often come slowly over months and years.

Rene again was dealing with the survivor's guilt of why he hadn't been there to do more. He asked himself how he could have better prepared this team for the very moment they would need it. He describes seeing his friend in such horrible physical condition that he prayed God would end the suffering for him and his family. He knew the road ahead would be long, and quite possibly it would end in death, regardless of the medical care his friend received to temporarily prolong his life. The burden on his family might be overwhelming; perhaps it would be easier to deal with his death rather than a life that would be forever altered. Most people will never face these kinds of struggles; if they do, they likely are not facing them while putting in sixteen-hour days and risking their lives with frequent combat engagements against an enemy that would like nothing more than to kill them in the most painful way possible.

Amazingly, God answered Rene's prayers by not providing the outcome nearly everyone believed to be a forgone conclusion. God chose instead to turn what was certain to be a devastating tragedy into a blessing that has inspired thousands to overcome the difficult circumstances they face and achieve more than they could have imagined. With the help of prosthetic legs and a cane, Rene's friend is now able to walk. Although medically retired from the Army, he continues to serve his community and is an advocate for veterans in Minnesota and across the country. The injury deeply affected

Rene, but so did the fight this soldier put forth as well as his long road to recovery. Incidents such as this IED detonation cannot always be avoided; however, the ability to survive these incidents increases proportionally with the quality of training one has received. The better the training, the greater the chances are for survival. While it's impossible to measure the success of the training Rene has provided over the years, it is fair to say that he has had a tremendous impact not only on this soldier but also on thousands of others. Rene continues to serve *in* honor of these soldiers but also *with* honor because of everything he has learned on his journey.

The one thing I have not discussed about Rene is his specific career field. I avoided this topic for good reason; the simple mention of what he does will bring abundant stereotypes to readers' minds, and they may read the rest of what I wrote about him through a lens that is dramatically skewed. Rene is one of a select few in a very exclusive community in the military: he is an Army Special Operator. He has served in numerous roles which cannot be disclosed, including as a Sniper. This is not *who* he is, though; he is so much more. He is the heart and soul of "not your average Joe." He became a member of an elite unit because of his talents, but he is a soldier because of his core values. He put this to the test during his selection training to become a Special Operator, which the title of this chapter, "The Licorice Test," refers to. Near the end of this training, he was responsible for a team in the field and was called over to a group of instructors. Field conditions are never easy; they are even more difficult when the training is as physically demanding as this was and performed with a few hours of sleep over the course of a week. Even though the team is tired and hungry, they'll keep going no matter the obstacle even while they dream of a decent meal and a warm bed. When Rene reported to the instructors, they were all sitting around eating licorice. They asked him if he would like a piece. At this point he was tired, hungry, and thinking only somewhat clearly, mostly operating on automatic pilot. Not surprisingly he accepted the offer. It is what he did next that is the epitome of honor. He went back to his team, took out his knife, and cut the licorice into equal pieces so all the members of the team could have a piece. His instinct was not to take the treat only for himself but to care for all those under his care. None of this happened by chance; Rene had forged his core

The True Test of Honor - The Licorice Test

values through his military service, and the instructors used this simple test to measure both the man and his values. He did not waver in his response and passed the test.

During the Memorial Day service in 2012, Rene again displayed the sense of honor that has come to define him. As is customary of military members in dress uniform, we take notice of decorations that others wear. I noticed Rene wearing a Bronze Star with a "V" device, which recognized valorous service. He displayed many other decorations, but I realized one of his decorations was missing: the Purple Heart. Knowing he had earned it, I asked him why he did not have it displayed. I learned he had earned not one Purple Heart but three. His response humbled me to my core. He recalled the incident detailed earlier in this chapter where one of his own lost both of his legs. Rene admitted he had been wounded but that his friend had lost his legs; as long as Rene had his legs and could walk, he would not wear his Purple Hearts. I can think of no better way to define honor than the way Rene defines it and lives it daily.

Corporate Application

Honor is a value that in part is the thread that weaves an intricate tapestry of all core values into a piece that is deeply meaningful to all who view it. Without honor, would integrity, excellence, leadership, vision, or any other value weave the same tapestry? Would the message be the same? What impact would honor have in your company if all employees shared this value? What measurable and sustainable ROI (return on investment) would it create for your organization, and how would you put metrics into place to measure it? What impact would honoring your customers have on revenue, profitability, and customer retention? What if employees honored one another with all they did? If leaders honored employees at all levels in the organization, what effect would this have on productivity and morale?

Veteran Application

If you are a veteran, when have you displayed honor? What were the circumstances in which you displayed honor? When answering this or any other potential interview question, use a technique known as the STAR method (Situation, Task, Action, and Results). When you are interviewing for a job, it isn't enough to simply say you have core values such as honor; you must clearly define them. The best assumption you can make as a candidate is that your interviewer knows little about what you have done and even less the culture you come from. If core values are the tapestry that defines military service, weave the tapestry in such a way that the interviewer simply cannot ignore the values you bring with you to employment beyond the military. Make sure that your audience easily understands your examples and that they are measurable and relevant. Core values begin and end with honor; they are relevant and can be measured. Your job as a candidate is to communicate this to your audience.

The True Test of Honor - The Licorice Test

Rene and his team on a mission in Kosovo, 2004

Rene and his boys, Noah and Zachary, before he leaves for Iraq, 2006

The True Test of Honor - The Licorice Test

Rene passing the time in Iraq painting a mural commemorating 9-11

"Have the courage to say no. Have the courage to face the truth. Do the right thing because it is right. These are the magic keys to living your life with integrity."

- W. Clement Stone, businessman, philanthropist, author

Chapter 2
Kenny Rogers's *The Gambler* Equals Integrity?

In 1978 Kenny Rogers released "The Gambler." The song soared to number one on the country chart and climbed as high as sixteen on the pop chart, long before the recent overlap of pop and country genres. The chorus goes like this.

> You got to know when to hold 'em, know when to fold 'em,
>
> know when to walk away and know when to run.
>
> You never count your money when you're sittin' at the table.
>
> There'll be time enough for countin' when the dealin's done.

If integrity is defined as adhering to moral and ethical principles—in other words, having moral character and being honest—how do the lyrics of "The Gambler" apply? Much of the attention given to integrity focuses on behavioral responses that become automatic when one faces any given situation. While integrity is crucial to moral character, it also encompasses values such as discipline, courage, and the persistence to continue through even the most difficult of circumstances to complete a task. True integrity, though, is not only about persevering through difficult times; when done right it should resemble the lyrics in "The Gambler." At times the only way to get something done right is to know when to walk away or when to run and have the integrity to admit that this is exactly what is required. This is a lesson Kristen Maloney has learned firsthand during her fourteen plus years of service in the Air Force Reserve.

As is the case with many who serve, Kristen enlisted with a set of values upon which the military could build, values her family instilled during her childhood in Minnesota. She comes from a large extended family and learned very early that freedom is a precious resource that must be protected. Her grandmother immigrated to the United States from another country at a very early age to marry a man who already had been chosen for her. She found herself in a completely foreign culture that presented challenges; perhaps the most difficult of these was communicating in a language other than her native tongue. Large families were common in those days, and Kristen's grandparents had six children. If being an immigrant who speaks no English upon arrival, getting married and parenting six children wasn't difficult enough, Kristen's grandmother's husband died when five of the children were still school age. Through all of this, her grandmother persevered and loved her new country and the freedom she had by simply living in the United States. This was clearly something she fostered in her children and passed along to her grandchildren and beyond. This love of freedom and knowing it comes with a price were driving factors in Kristen's decision to serve her country in the Air Force.

Kristen attended college immediately following high school but really didn't have much in the way of a specific direction. College seemed like the natural next step, so she had taken the step. She attended classes on and off for five years but found herself not making progress toward any kind of a goal. In 1998 she took the oath of enlistment and left for basic training. The journey through basic training is always challenging and pushes individuals beyond what they believe their capabilities to be; Kristen's was further complicated as she entered the service as a single mother and her training required separation from her daughter. Taking life lessons from her grandmother, she paid the price for her freedom and proudly completed both basic and follow on technical training. Her discipline in staying strong has stayed with her in the nine plus years I have known her, and it is something she seeks to pass along to her children and to those with whom she serves. This trait has shown itself many times since basic training, most significantly when she returned to finish her bachelor's degree in business. While working full time and serving in the reserves approximately forty hours a month, she also raised her children and took a full course load beginning in 2007 until she graduated in 2009. While many people could not be bothered to make the sacrifices needed to accomplish a goal such as this, Kristen took the road less traveled and was successful doing so. Why did she do it? The reward was greater than the sacrifice, and she had the ability to do it. It not only made her more valuable as an employee but also made her a better parent and an example for her children regarding the sacrifices needed to realize one's dreams. It also has made her a much more effective mentor for younger service members who need encouragement to stand firm during difficult times. While this experience does not meet the traditional definition of integrity, it is integrity nonetheless. Others would have walked away, perhaps even run; Kristen stood firm, knew she held a winning hand, and did not fold.

Kristen has made herself known as a leader who is able to get things done; she has held leadership roles as early as during technical school immediately after basic training. She progressed through the junior enlisted ranks before being promoted to Senior Airman (E-4) and was one of the first reservists ever to be selected to attend Airman Leadership School with her active duty counterparts at Grand Forks Air Force Base. She has attended or taken multiple leadership and professional development classes, but it is this first course she gives credit for allowing her to start to build a leadership tool chest she still uses today both in and out of the military. As a Senior Airman, she was placed on active orders and served as the first ever Honor Guard Director at the 934th Airlift Wing in Minneapolis, MN. Leading an Honor Guard is an enormous responsibility that is not entrusted to just anyone, especially someone so junior in rank and time in service. Kristen not only accepted the responsibility but also thrived in everything she did, as she led teams that rendered final honors for veterans who had earned them. Ten years later the team is still going strong and is a true testament to the foundation she laid years earlier.

Kristen always has had a strong desire to serve not just her country but also others, wherever and whenever she can. Whether leading or following, mentoring or being mentored, she constantly seeks to make a difference in the lives of others. The most visible way she has achieved this is through serving as a member of the Wing Honor Guard. They spend countless hours preparing to represent the Air Force at various events or honor deceased veterans as they are laid to rest. With every event she attended, she served others as an ambassador of the Air Force and displayed the core values to which they subscribe. While service on the Honor Guard was meaningful for both Kristen and those she served, the most impactful moments in her career have come through service in ways the public will never see. Kristen is part of a small group of people who have done some of the most difficult work in the entire military: caring for our nation's fallen heroes through service at the military's central mortuary facility at Dover Air Force Base in Delaware. Those who serve there follow three simple words with every task they perform, Dignity, Honor and Respect. For almost everyone who serves there, this has become a theme in their lives long after their service at the mortuary ends.

Since 2000, Kristen has deployed four separate times, each time to the mortuary at Dover. Early in her career as a very young airman, she answered the call to join the team responsible for processing the remains of nineteen marines killed during the April 8, 2000 V-22 Osprey crash in Arizona. There is never an easy time to begin working at the mortuary; an aircraft crash with nineteen casualties is one of the most difficult situations one could be called in on. While her first experience was challenging, her second deployment, in the days following the terrorist attacks of September 11, 2001, was infinitely more difficult. Usually the military would not be involved in processing remains for such incidents, but that changed instantly when the Pentagon was attacked and the remains of 125 casualties needed to be identified and returned to the families as quickly as possible. The hours were long, and the mission was difficult, perhaps the most difficult of any the military has to offer. It is grueling work mentally, physically, and emotionally. What happens there truly stays there and is closely guarded information; even if those who serve there could discuss it with people outside those four walls, few would comprehend the nature of the work that is done there.

Kristen deployed two more times after 9/11, in 2004 and 2005-6. In 2005 I had the privilege of being deployed to the mortuary with her. These were very busy times, with some of the highest casualty rates seen during Operation IRAQI FREEDOM. I was proud to see the way Kristen not only did her job but also stepped forward every time she had an opportunity to lead others and set an example for them to follow. The first time she deployed to Dover, she felt tremendous anxiety about the mission and getting everything right; the one thing the mission does not allow for is mistakes. While the anxiety diminishes over time, it never completely goes away. During each subsequent deployment to Dover, she was confident in her abilities, but the anxiety remained; she knew the job she was about to undertake was the result of tragedy in the life of another. Through these unique experiences, she was challenged beyond where she thought she was capable of going and learned quickly that the world is bigger than she is. Suddenly the little things that bothered her before weren't quite as important or significant, considering the loss and devastation she saw daily. In short it gave her an entirely different perspective on life, one she carries with her to this day. She feels tremendous pride regarding what she contributed while at Dover, a pride tempered by the humility that came with the mission. Caring for our nation's fallen is a poignant lesson in selfless service, as those they serve, the fallen and their families, have demonstrated the ultimate sacrifice of selfless service. Kristen applies these lessons in her continued Air Force service, in how she raises her children, and in her career in the private sector.

Kristen subscribes to a whole-person concept, as she seeks to continue to build her leadership tool chest. From her time at the mortuary as well as a variety of other assignments, to continuing leadership and professional development courses she has completed, she uses her core values to make her a better leader. When she leaves the base, her leadership does not end. Kristen tries just as hard with her civilian employer and her kids to lead by example and be the best person she can be in all situations. She constantly looks to build in others the values she has learned while doing all she can to develop those around her in meaningful ways. She knows she has been fortunate over the course of her career to be exposed to fantastic mentors who invested a great deal in her; she simply wants to pay that forward as often as possible.

Kristen's concept of integrity also includes being fair and honest with those she leads or serves with and remaining consistent in her actions while navigating through difficult or adverse environments. While serving at the mortuary can be tremendously difficult, it also provides unique opportunities for growth many never will experience during their careers. Kristen learned very early that these missions allow absolutely no room for a lack of integrity; when mistakes are made, intentional or not, they cannot be rescinded and can have a lifelong impact on a grieving family. Speed of executing the mission at Dover matters, but not as much as getting it right no matter how long it takes. Attention to detail is of the utmost importance; every portion of human remains that comes through the doors at Dover is assigned an identification number and tracked at all times. Every effort is made to properly identify *all* remains and return them to the family.

Kristen recalls a time when the mission required very long hours; she had worked for days with few breaks and very little sleep. Yet the mission demanded more, and while she had little left to give, she refused to give up; her integrity to the mission and the families she served would keep her going. A positive identification came back on a portion that had been placed in storage until it could be identified. She was assigned to retrieve the portion so the process could be finished and the family could have closure. Hours passed as Kristen searched for the portion. She checked, double-checked, and even triple-checked, yet she could not find it anywhere. If she could not find the portion, it would mean a huge breech of integrity for the storage processes at Dover, and the implications would be far reaching. She had to find it, so the search continued; yet the harder she looked, the more stress she put herself under to find it. When she could look no further and was absolutely convinced it was nowhere to be found, she prepared herself to break the news to her supervisor and inform him that the portion had been lost. As one would expect, the reaction was less than pleasant. He immediately proceeded to the storage area, accompanied by Kristen, to verify that it was indeed missing. Within minutes he located the portion, exactly where it was supposed to be. It was at that moment she realized she had compromised her integrity. While the error hadn't been malicious or intentional, she had made a mistake in what was supposed to be an error free game.

Never one to give up, Kristen kept going long after she should have in order to complete the mission. Through all of this, she learned a valuable lesson about integrity: true integrity does not merely focus on moral character but also on honesty with yourself and others, honesty that steps forward to admit that continuing on the assigned task will cause the team more harm than good and might needlessly compromise integrity. She needed help, and not admitting that fact to others gave failure an opportunity to rear its ugly head. In the end all worked out with the portion being found, but it did not have to happen this way. Kristen carries this lesson with her and shares it with others in an effort to mentor them regarding how to avoid the pitfalls into which she sometimes has fallen.

In the private sector, Kristen works as a manager for a federal contractor, where she leads a diverse team that interacts with internal customers across the United States. Drawing on her years of real world leadership experience and the tool chest she has assembled, she recently found herself in a delicate situation as a manager. The organization was downsizing and slowly eliminating positions to gradually reduce the workforce prior to making major changes with the remainder of the workforce hitting the streets as operations in Minnesota are shuttered. In many ways this is a lose-lose proposition for any manager; the jobs were going away, and for most there would be no silver lining. Kristen was tasked with eliminating a specific headcount on her team, and the choice was hers regarding who to eliminate. Just as she had learned at Dover, there are two sides to the integrity coin, and she needed to pay attention to both sides. On the front side, there was an accepted practice in place that took seniority into account, so regardless of performance the last one hired into the department would be the first one out. On the back side, these cuts were real and they affected real people with real lives, families, and financial obligations. Many times the back side of the coin gives way to the front side in an effort to be fair but often falls far short of true fairness. So how did Kristen apply integrity in this case? She evaluated the entire picture and sought to turn a lose-lose situation into a win-win for those she managed. One of the more senior team members already had another position to fall back on and was waiting until his position was officially eliminated before he moved on. Kristen also knew there was another member of the team with less seniority who did not have another position to go to. This team member was a single parent. Being let go would impact both members, but clearly it would affect the latter far more significantly than the former. Kristen made the only choice she felt she could; she eliminated the position held by the member who had another position lined up. She made the decision based on all the information available to her rather than the limited data typically available in these circumstances. She did not stop there; she went to her team and explained the entire situation, why she had made her decision, and how it benefited all members of the team. She calmed any fears that existed about future eliminations; her team knew that her integrity would not be compromised and that she would treat all of them fairly. It was another powerful lesson in not just playing the hand Kristen was dealt but in playing it correctly. Integrity is not simply a call to action; it is a call to take the appropriate action at the correct time. This is precisely what she did.

Kristen continues to enjoy her service and the diversity of experiences it provides her. She has given a great deal in service to her country and has been rewarded beyond her wildest expectations; it has positively affected who she is as a person, a mother, and an employee. Since entering the service more than a decade ago, she has grown and developed into a complete package. She has become highly skilled and very well rounded through both military and civilian education, various technical and professional development courses, and positions of tremendous responsibility she held much earlier in her career than her peers did outside the service. Few if any other careers offer opportunities for such growth and development; she has been fortunate to have taken advantage of opportunities nearly every time they present themselves. At first she knew nothing about how to do the jobs she eventually would be assigned during her career, but the military gave her all the tools she needed, and through this she has been successful at everything she has been asked to do. Although she did not go into her current role in the private sector with extensive experience, in short order she took what she was given and not only survived but also thrived, as she continually took on more responsibility. Identifying and hiring the right veterans in any company will elevate team performance and results while enhancing the values of the organization. Kristen is one of many who are living proof of this.

Corporate Application

Does your company culture focus on an integrity that calls for employees to always "hold" or is it a culture that welcomes "fold," "walk," and "run" when appropriate? Do you give your employees freedom to make decisions based on the values of the organization as well as the latitude to make the right decisions based on the circumstances at hand versus what the manual says one should do? What would your organization look like if your employees shared these values and desired the results that came with unquestionable integrity? What would it mean to your customers, employee morale, revenue, profits, and the impact your company has on the communities where it has a presence? Pursuing sustainable veteran hiring initiatives can provide this and much more.

Veteran Application

Have you been pushed to a breaking point that caused you to do things that under normal circumstances you would not have done? How did you learn from this, and how did it affect your integrity as you moved forward? Have you ever made a decision that was not looked upon favorably, but afterward you realized integrity was clearly a factor in your decision and the results were vastly more favorable than they would have been had you taken the road typically traveled by others? Companies need employees who can stand on their own and make decisions with little to no supervision. They desperately need integrity in the decision making process, whether it means standing up and taking action or holding off because that is what the situation warrants. As a veteran you should clearly possess this kind of integrity. Are you capable of citing documentable examples of how you have displayed integrity in your decision making process? Communicating this will demonstrate your value as a potential employee and exponentially increase your chances of being hired. Know your value and be able to articulate it.

Kristen and parents at Airman Leadership School graduation

Kristen and parents after graduation ceremony, 2009

Kenny Rogers's The Gambler Equals Integrity?

Kristen and children, 2012

"The selfless actions of these heroes have removed them from their families, businesses, and homeland to fight, so that others may experience the liberty awaiting our troops upon safe return to America."

- Jim Walsh, former New York State representative

Chapter 3
Selfless Service - There is No "I" in Team

★

Helen Lester authored a children's book titled *Me First*, a story of a pig named Pinkerton who opts for selfishness in all he does. When given the opportunity to live a "me first" life, he learns a valuable lesson on why being first is not always best. The "me first" attitude typifies what has become the norm in American society, as the media and Hollywood constantly glamorize the selfish actions of athletes and public figures. The star wide receiver tweets that he isn't getting the ball thrown his way frequently enough. The star basketball player complains that he doesn't get enough shots at the basket and could score many more points if his teammates would let him. The famous actor bickers that nothing is ever good enough, especially when he is forced to wait at the airport for a flight, for a seat at his favorite restaurant, or for the valet to bring his car around. Selfishness has become a way of life that makes a story of service - selfless service - all the more amazing. Selfless service is precisely the story of Air Force Senior Master Sergeant Roy "Rex" Smith.

Rex grew up in a small town in northern Illinois as the fifth of six children. He comes from humble beginnings, with both parents having worked in a factory during his childhood. Rex was your typical small town American boy, active in the community and an accomplished athlete who played football, basketball, and baseball. After graduation he attended a small community college, and like many other students, he worked his way through school.

While he enjoyed school and wanted to progress toward his degree, he wasn't quite ready to be a full-time college student. Looking for some direction in his life, he considered the option of military service. He went to the Marine Corps recruiting office, and as is the case in many smaller communities, it was co-located with the other branches of service. The Marine recruiter was out of the office at a lunch appointment, so Rex waited. The Air Force recruiter was present and struck up a conversation with him. After a short discussion about all the options the Air Force had to offer, Rex decided to enlist in the Air Force. He began his service in January 1993 and was excited to start his career in Security Forces, what most people outside the Air Force would consider military police. As with even the best laid plans, unexpected detours can change the course of your life forever. Rex hit just such a detour. During a physical, a doctor determined that his vision was fine for serving in the Air Force but did not meet the standard for Security Forces, so Rex was forced to choose another career field. He chose what at the time was known as Services, a diverse career field that focused on food service, lodging, fitness centers, and strangely enough, mortuary affairs. He spent the next four years on active duty, deploying four times, three to Saudi Arabia and once to Guantanamo Bay, Cuba.

After leaving active duty, Rex began his career in the Air Force Reserve in 1997. He spent a year in Texas serving, working part time, and going to school, before family needs led him closer to home in 1998. He continued to serve at the 440th Airlift Wing in Milwaukee, Wisconsin, before a base closure forced his transfer to Minneapolis, where he has been since 2006. He's held a variety of positions in a variety of fields during the past twenty years, including food service, both in the kitchen and storeroom; fitness and recreation; equipment maintenance; lodging; readiness; and training. Over the years he has held various leadership roles and currently serves as Superintendent for approximately forty personnel, acting as an advisor to senior squadron leadership and a liaison to the enlisted corps, ensuring all personnel training is either met or exceeded.

Rex is proud of his service, not as much for what he has accomplished but for what he feels he has been able to give back to others. Over the past

Selfless Service - There is No "I" in Team

twenty years, he has faced his share of challenges, with supervisors who seemed to be more interested in serving themselves than others as well as a base closure in Milwaukee. At one point he considered stepping away from military life all together, but he is grateful he did not. He was fortunate to have a mentor encourage him to stay. The mentor saw great potential in him, potential that Rex could not see as he was too caught up in the daily grind of what he was doing. Looking back over the years, he can see how much he has developed both personally and professionally. More important, as he has gained both rank and responsibility, he has been rewarded with greater opportunities to mentor and develop others; he shares what so many have taken the time to share with him. When asked to name his accomplishments, he speaks about investing in others, which in no small way has contributed to his career longevity and success.

While highlights of his career come quickly to mind, one topic comes up just as quickly when Rex is asked about the disappointments he may have. He says he has no regrets, but if he could change one thing, he would have stayed in school and finished his four-year degree. Although he had some challenging family issues, he did not maintain enough discipline to either work through these or to take a short amount of time off before returning to earn his degree. He did obtain an associate's degree in hotel, restaurant, and fitness management but did not progress any further. Turning a negative into a positive, Rex looks for every opportunity he can to tell those he mentors, and anyone else who will listen, never to waste an opportunity to better themselves. He goes even further and encourages others not to simply wait for growth to come to them but to go out and seek it. When facing challenging times, he says, persevere and keep making progress toward your goal. His advice is powerful, as he did not achieve his goal; while it is never too late to realize a dream, his life circumstances are such that it is not practical for him to return to school. It is these life lessons Rex shares freely with others that make him an effective leader and mentor.

Unquestionably the hallmark of Rex's career has been selfless service. Once he settled on his choice for a career field in the Air Force, he became particularly interested in an often overlooked area of the field, mortuary affairs.

Less than a year out of basic training, Rex was first exposed to this portion of the career field as personnel in the squadron responded to a suicide while he was on his first deployment. It wasn't something he had any relevant experience doing, but it was nevertheless deeply meaningful to him. On his second deployment, a coalition aircraft crashed, and he was again part of the team that was called on for recovery of the remains of the pilot. The crash happened at night, and the team was immediately notified; however, recovery did not begin until the next morning. It was a very long and sleepless night. Early the next morning the team was gathered and briefed regarding the mission details; shortly after first light, they began the long and arduous task of retrieving the remains of the deceased pilot. It was a painstaking process undertaken in extreme conditions with temperatures well in excess of one hundred degrees. In mortuary work there is no margin for error. *All* human remains and personal effects must be recovered; to do anything less is considered a failure. The terrain where the crash happens can further complicate recovery efforts. In this case the terrain was flat; however, it was made up primarily of sand and gravel, and littered with debris from the crash.

The team spent the entire day searching. As daylight drew to a close, leadership determined they had recovered all remains and the mission would be suspended. A short while later, word came from leadership that the family had been contacted and two key personal effects were missing from the crash. What may seem trivial meant everything for the family, so the search resumed. Portable lights were called in so the search could continue even as darkness set in. After several more hours of searching and more than eighteen total hours of arduous work, the team recovered the items after sifting through the sand and gravel one small load at a time. Leadership again suspended the search then notified the family that they had recovered the items. Although this would not bring back their loved one, it did provide some closure. Rex learned a valuable lesson that stifling hot day in the desert: do unto others as you would have them do unto you; the best way to accomplish this is through selfless service. The team had wanted to quit; they had found enough, and it would have been easy to send word that they simply could not find the missing items. After all, the plane had crashed and much of it had disintegrated on impact. Of the two items they had searched for, one was a

SELFLESS SERVICE - THERE IS NO "I" IN TEAM

wedding band the pilot always had with him. They weren't looking for a needle in a haystack but might as well have been, a gold ring in a sand and gravel pit is just as hard to find. But they did find it. This experience was a lesson in selfless service that Rex carries with him to this day.

While mortuary work is deeply meaningful duty, it is a duty no one ever hopes to have. For one to be called to duty, a tragedy has to have taken place, meaning someone has died. Rex never could have imagined the next major incident for which he would be called to assist and help lead recovery efforts. Serving in Saudi Arabia, he was housed just a few buildings away from Khobar Towers Building 131 in June 1996. His normal routine was to work out and run in the evening, which he did, but that night he had to cut his run short. He had cleaned up and was already in his room when just before 10:00 p.m. a truck bomb detonated approximately seventy feet from building 131, leaving a crater eight feet wide and thirty five feet deep while destroying the entire front face of the tower. The incident left nineteen people dead and hundreds wounded. After a night of no sleep and knowing what the morning would bring, Rex and the rest of the team were briefed and began the gruesome task of recovery for the nineteen casualties. This time the recovery did not involve sifting through sand for personal effects; instead it took place in an unstable building littered with hazards every step of the way. The teams moved room by room, floor by floor, for several days until the last of the nineteen was accounted for. Rex was on the team that recovered the nineteenth and final casualty.

Rex's previous experience in recovery had been for a pilot he had not known. While it's never easy to separate yourself completely from the mission at hand, some recoveries are easier than others. Khobar Towers was not one of the easier missions. During his normal duty, Rex worked at the fitness center. In one way or another, he had met and associated with each one of the casualties at Khobar Towers. Some he knew better than others, but he had a tie with each of them. Even so, Rex had a job to do, and this time it was very personal. The process of removing remains has changed somewhat over the years; at this time it was much like an episode of *CSI*. Work began in the field, with Rex and others gathering fingerprints and assisting in positively identifying the remains before they were shipped to the mortuary at Dover Air Force Base. The sights, sounds, smells, and actual process of handling human remains has left an indelible mark on Rex, a burden he must bear the rest of his life. After the recovery was complete, he remained with the FBI to assist in the recovery of evidence related to the bombing. Even though the remains were gone, the reminders were still there and the task no less difficult. One thought replayed itself in Rex's head: *if this happened to me, what would I want others to do to get me home to my family?* Rex also wanted to do whatever he could do to contribute to building a case against the perpetrators. No matter how difficult the task at hand, he always has answered the call; his efforts in recovery of remains epitomize the true definition of selfless service.

While nothing Rex does in his career beyond the military will bring the same gravity and life-changing experiences, he carries these same core values with him and applies them with the same discipline in the work he does today. For several years he has worked for the Department of Transportation in the state in which he lives, and each year the department hired temporary workers to help during peak seasons. Most others let these employees fend for themselves; no one helped them when they were hired as a temp so why should they go out of their way to help others? Rex, however, uses the values he has forged over the years to serve these new hires, putting their needs above his own for the good of the team and the entire community. Rex and his coworkers drive large equipment, and safety is their highest priority, both their own safety and that of the general public. Rex always has gone out of his way to train each new hire as thoroughly as he can, giving them a great deal of experience with each ride they take with him. There are those who don't care to listen, but most times they absorb everything he can give them and frequently call him when they are on their own to ask for advice regarding situations they encounter. While Rex isn't in a direct supervisory role, he is always willing to go the extra mile for anyone on the team and mentor as often as he can; he lives selfless service without regard for the reward or what might be in it for him.

As my interview with Rex came to a close, he had some final thoughts to share. Looking back on his twenty years of service, he has seen great diversity in those with whom he has worked. Whether on active duty or reserve status, serving at his home station or deployed overseas, those he served with came from nearly every walk of life prior to entering military service. It is these differences that made a very strong and unique team that he saw perform at locations around the world. All the values he has learned are directly pertinent to the job he now does outside of the military, and he is grateful for the growth he has experienced over the years. Few careers provide the opportunity to develop these core values; companies expect employees to show up with these values, yet many new hires fall short in this area. Since one cannot learn these values just anywhere, if a company is looking to build a team around critical core values, Rex believes it should give strong consideration to how it can employ more veterans. Rex's experience is anything but average, and his values demonstrate he is anything but an average Joe.

Corporate Application

Does your organization have a culture of selfless service, or is its culture more closely aligned with *selfish* service? What impact does selfish service have on workforce morale? What effect does it have on customers, revenues, and shareholder return? If your culture models *selfishness* rather than selfless service, does the organization have a plan to change this? If so, how? Does the plan incorporate changes in hiring strategies to reflect a more values-centric approach and to promote the hiring of employees who are a strong value match? If so, how do veterans fit into this plan? Do you have a vision to hire more veterans as well as a metric-driven, strategic, executable hiring plan that will lead to the changes your company seeks?

Veteran Application

For nearly forty years now, the US military has been an all-volunteer force. By raising your hand and taking the oath of enlistment, you have committed one of the most selfless acts. With service comes an inherent risk that may, at any time, require you to lay your life down for another service member or simply to protect the freedom of all Americans. While few are called to make this ultimate sacrifice, raising your hand acknowledges this risk and demonstrates that you are committed to pay this price should it be required of you. Most veterans not only serve while on duty but also serve in the community and look for ways to expand their sphere of influence by volunteering their time and resources to those in need. As a veteran, do you have practical and tangible examples of this service? Can you quantify this service and define the benefit of this service to the community? Consider not only stateside community service but also what have you volunteered to do while serving or while deployed overseas in a foreign culture. This service may be performed in the community beyond the gates of the base, but it also can be associated with those in need within the military community through organizations such as Wounded Warrior. All of this service brings value to an organization. Work to clearly define what you have accomplished beyond your daily responsibilities. Finally, how have you contributed to the success of a team through the mentoring and development of others? All of these examples speak to selfless service and provide value to any organization. Find ways to demonstrate how you have selflessly served others.

Unloading produce in Kuwait, 2002

SELFLESS SERVICE - THERE IS NO "I" IN TEAM

Deployed to Saudi Arabia, 1996, pictured with friend Mike Beck

"We are what we repeatedly do. Excellence, then, is not an act, but a habit."

- Aristotle

Chapter 4
Excel – Not Just a Spreadsheet but Also a Core Value?

Veterans list a variety of reasons for why they joined the military. One fairly common answer is that they lacked a purpose or direction in life and felt the military could provide this. In most cases the military delivers exactly what is needed, as it builds character, discipline, and a desire to excel in all that one does. These values last a lifetime and are directly transferable to any employer outside of the military. The story of Dave Hardy clearly demonstrates the growth that is fostered through military service. One would be hard pressed to find a better colleague, supervisor, friend, and mentor.

Dave began his career in 1983 as a twenty-three-year old who wanted to serve but did not have the focus in life he was looking for. After graduating from high school, he tried several different professional options, but none of them really appealed to him. He spent a year at a small junior college but was only there to play football. A month into the school year, the team disbanded because it had barely enough members to field a team. Once football ended, Dave saw no reason to put in the time required to complete his coursework; at the time, he felt college just wasn't for him. He tried life in California for less than a year before returning to Minnesota and investing two years to obtain a diesel mechanic certification. He ultimately discovered that while he was good at being a mechanic, he didn't want to make a career out of it after being called to fix a piece of heavy equipment in minus-forty degree weather. He remembered an Army recruiter visiting his high school and discussing options with the students, but at the time he felt it wasn't a fit for him. Now several years removed from high school and with no clear direction in life, Dave again considered military service; further investigation with recruiters led him to the Air Force, and he shipped off to basic training within two months.

Dave grew up in St. Paul, Minnesota, before moving to the small town of Nashwauk in the northern part of the state. Being older than the average enlistee gave him a unique opportunity to be immediately placed into leadership positions. He also quickly learned just how small the brotherhood of military service is. While working with a counselor to choose his career field, he was asked if he was indeed from the small town of Nashwauk. To his amazement, the counselor was also from the same small town, and they had extended family members who knew one another. For Dave this experience became the first of many examples of how you take care of others. He didn't receive any special treatment, nor was he accepted into a career field for which he wasn't qualified, but there was a connection there, and the counselor wanted to make sure Dave was taken care of. Eventually this became one of the hallmarks of Dave's career, always taking care of the needs of others when you have the ability to do so; he is one of the most selfless people I have ever met.

Dave selected a career in electronics and the emerging specialty of computer networks. Between his initial technical training and follow on training, he spent the better part of his first year going through extensive training and certification in his new career. Although he was stationed in Florida, exercises took him to Korea and across the United States; during his four years of duty, he spent more time traveling than he spent at his home duty station. He transitioned off active duty service in 1987 and joined the Air Force Reserve in Minneapolis in 1988. He also transitioned to a new career field in

A Spreadsheet but Also a Core Value?

law enforcement, working in what was then known as Security Police and is now known as Security Forces. He excelled in this new career and the training associated with it; he completed his initial training as an honor graduate and set a standard of performance that would stay with him for the rest of his Air Force career and well beyond. Dave had the privilege of deploying for ongoing security operations in Panama and participating in numerous security details in support of visits from the President of the United States and one very unique visit to Minnesota in 1990 by the last General Secretary of the Communist Party of the Soviet Union, Mikhail Gorbachev.

Dave's most important value has been one of the Air Force's three core values, excellence in all he does. Few have been as consistent in their adherence to this core value as Dave. To say he is competitive would be an understatement; he wants to win in everything he does. His desire to win, however, is not tied to personal recognition; he would do even the most complicated and difficult tasks with the full knowledge that there was no possibility of recognition for his efforts. For him the reward and recognition come in knowing he has done the best he can every time he puts forth the effort to complete a task. Win or lose, excelling in all he does is the reward; when Dave does his best, the winning always has taken care of itself. He was such a valuable leader because he held his team to the same high standards, and they knew it. If Dave asked them to give their all, he would be right there beside them giving his all, which naturally translated to excellence in all they did both individually and as a team.

Dave faced a number of challenges throughout his career. His biggest professional challenge came when he was forty years old and received the opportunity to pursue a chance at becoming a member of an elite Air Force flyaway security team known as Ravens. Washout rates for this training are extraordinarily high; few expected him to make it through the school at forty years of age, let alone excel in the course. In typical Dave fashion, he did just that. The two-week training is grueling. Constant physical training in hand-to-hand combat techniques left him battered and bruised, yet he continued on. The course challenged its students mentally as well, as they were tested in deescalating a wide variety of situations not just with their hands but also their brains and a variety of verbal judo techniques. They were trained to handle any security situation for whatever airframe they were flying on. Missions were all across the globe and often to remote, austere airstrips with little or no local security support, limited communication capabilities, and usually a less than friendly reception from those in the area. Cultures were different at every location where they landed, as were the languages spoken. The mission was either to deliver much needed cargo and personnel or to pick up precious human cargo, usually in the form of a terrorist, which the locals sometimes weren't eager to see depart the area. They operated in small teams with enormous responsibilities; foreign relations could be affected during every single mission. Ravens only select the very best, those who excel in everything they do; failure is never an option. In 2000 Dave became Raven 571 and began a journey that would take him around the world many times over, a journey that would only intensify after September 11, 2001.

After September 11th, US military security posture around the world went from zero to sixty in a matter of hours. Shortly after the planes hit the towers, members of the Ravens received calls informing them that they would be activated. Given his experience and specialized skills, Dave knew the call would come and immediately began to pack for activation at an unknown location and for an undetermined period of time. Dave and his team began in Minneapolis, providing local security, then worked in Washington State before traveling overseas to work a variety of missions. They continued to train along the way. Dave became Air Marshall qualified and completed training known as SERE (survival, evasion, resistance, and escape) in the small Arab country of Qatar. There was a constant learning curve, as each mission took them to a country and culture they may never have been in and presented its own unique set of challenges. The list of locations Dave has traveled to reads like the pages of a world atlas, with visits to Guam, Russia, Djibouti, Eritrea, Ethiopia, Kenya, Afghanistan, Pakistan, South Africa, Diego Garcia, Chile, Columbia, Ecuador, Peru, Haiti, and many other places. The missions were as varied as the locations he visited, and he performed a wide range of duties, from escorting Embassy and United

A Spreadsheet but Also a Core Value?

Nations personnel in and out of these countries to transporting detainees off the battlefield and into US custody halfway around the world.

In addition to the excellence Dave displays in his own performance, his success is also directly tied to the performance of his team members. Dave realized long ago that the easiest way to achieve maximum effort and performance in a team environment is to take care of those with whom he served. When they were on a mission, the team checked into the local lodging facility while Dave found food and learned the times and availability of food service support and any other services his team required. Regardless of what was needed, Dave always took care of his team. He gave those on his team who were junior to him in rank the opportunity to excel and contribute their own special skills to whatever situation they faced.

In 2003 I began my career in the Air Force Reserve, and Dave was one of the first people I met. From the very first moment, I knew he cared about others and would put his own interests aside if he could help another develop his or her skills or career. In short he always did what he could to invest in others. One duty weekend I was scheduled for training in use of force techniques and various methods for disarming and apprehending a suspect. Given Dave's expertise in this area, he easily could have taken the approach that he knew everything and that we were there to learn from him. Instead he recognized the professional experience I brought, which differed from his, and asked me to help him facilitate the training. To Dave the value others received from the training was more important than who received the credit for teaching it. Knowing the team would benefit, he shared credit for the training. It is lessons like these in taking care of your team and those around you that I carry with me to this day. My success is in part due to the mentorship I received from others, especially from times I spent directly with Dave. He taught me to always train and prepare for the opportunity to take on additional responsibility and face whatever might lie ahead. Not one to stand still, he believed a career should progress, and opportunities come to those who are prepared to take advantage of them. I have taken these lessons with me, and as I prepare others in the service for career transition, I counsel them on working to progress their career and to be prepared for whatever comes their way.

During his military career, Dave shared lessons about dealing with difficult times and emphasized that successful people always make the best of even the worst situations. Not long after meeting him, I faced such a situation; my wife was pregnant with our second child and lost the baby. This happened immediately prior to a duty weekend; the last place I wanted to be was at the base that weekend. Dave knew this and took the time to invest in me; he knew from experience how to make it through life's challenges.

While many others remember 2001 for the terrorist attacks that killed three thousand people, Dave has memories of an event that dramatically ratcheted up the pressure in an already stressful environment. His wife was diagnosed with breast cancer and faced a long road ahead, which included a battle to save her own life. Few could imagine leaving their family and putting their life on the line to defend the freedoms we take for granted. Even fewer could fathom doing so with a wife fighting a potentially deadly illness. Trusting God and depending on his network of family and friends to bridge the gap created in his absence, he answered the call and served with excellence and honor. I cannot thank him enough, nor will I ever forget the investment he has made in my life and career.

At various times in life, regardless of effort, there is very little one can do to change the situation they are facing. During these times what an individual is made of becomes clearly defined and shapes the response to such difficult times. In 2007 Dave faced nearly insurmountable challenges, and he had no control over the outcome. His wife of sixteen years was diagnosed for a second time with a different and very aggressive form of breast cancer that carried a five-year survival rate of less than 40 percent, half that of patients with less aggressive forms of breast cancer. While doing his best to keep a positive attitude and fight the good fight, Dave knew very little could be done and that their time as a family was limited to a matter of months. He learned the value of excellence in all he did through these very dark days; it wasn't a challenge one wins awards for based on performance. His family needed him, his wife needed him, and his employer needed him just as much

A Spreadsheet but Also a Core Value?

as he needed them to continue providing an income for his family. Each of them was like a leg on a stool, and without the right focus on each of them, the stool would become unbalanced and eventually collapse under its own weight. On some days the stool wobbled more than it did on others, but he did all he could to hold the stool together. While Dave could be a rock to stabilize the stool, he could not stop the cancer that consumed his wife; she lost her battle with cancer on October 11, 2007. I never will forget when he called to let me know the battle was over and to discuss the funeral with me. Without a second thought, I did exactly what Dave taught me to do; I reached out to help someone on the team in his time of need. I made the drive to northern Minnesota to stand with my friend and mentor. I have no doubt if the call came from me he would do the same.

Dave has applied the values he learned in the military directly to employment beyond the military. He has worked for the same manufacturing company in northern Minnesota for sixteen years. The firm has stood behind him through his service and life challenges, in part because his employers have known he is someone they always can count on to do the right thing to the best of his ability. Years ago he took over a safety program with little formal training to prepare him for the role. He had worked in construction, and through his military service, he certainly understood the impact safety has on a workplace. His predecessor held many other responsibilities, and there was little time left to focus on building a comprehensive safety program. So what did Dave do? He pulled in all the resources he could. He studied and learned OSHA and MN OSHA regulations that affected his company. He learned anything and everything he could and figured out how to get whatever he needed to get the job done. Most important, he has built a team of superior performers to whom he gives most of the credit for making safety a priority. The team has expanded the safety program from a single facility to all four North American facilities as well as one in Chile, one in Australia, and one in Mexico. Using the same leadership and team management skills he learned in the Air Force, results have consistently improved, which has impacted employees and customers alike. In his civilian career, he manages teams the same way he did in the military; he instills a sense of pride in what the employees are doing, takes care of them in any way he can, and teaches them the value of excelling in all they do. The results speak for themselves.

In 2004 Dave retired from the Air Force Reserve as a Master Sergeant (E-7). He is fortunate to have been with his employer for the last sixteen years, with much of that time overlapping his military career. He has seen his share of friends who have been casualties of the economy, with positions eliminated as their companies were forced to do more with less. He says he is grateful for the values he learned from the military as well as how those values directly affect the job he does every day. He sees the military as the best training ground to build these values in future employees. The military develops and fosters an attitude of constant teamwork and an environment where the needs of the team are willingly put ahead of the individual. He has served with and led some great teams, but they were only as good as the weakest member. The US military is the best in the world because they work to develop the weakest members and maximize the use of the strengths they offer. Everyone on the team strives to continually improve and hone their skills to the best they can be. Dave brings these values and more, but he is quick to share that most veterans bring the same values, regardless of the job title or rank they held while serving.

After reading Dave's story, it would be easy to see how he might be a negative person, perhaps believing the world owed him something, given all the challenges he has faced. He could be bitter, and as many do, try to drown his sorrows and bury the pain. Dave, however, is a realist but also extremely positive. He has been sober since 1982 and never gave a second thought to abandoning his sobriety to deal with his challenges. He has a strong faith that has carried him through the most difficult of his journeys. He knows his time with his family is limited, and he does all he can to take advantage of the time while he has it. Dave was fortunate to find love again and is now remarried. If you asked him for one word to describe his life, he would say he is blessed. Has he gone through painful times? Yes. Would he change any of them? Not a chance, they made him the person he is today, and he uses every opportunity to pass on his values to others. I am blessed for having known him. I proudly count him as a colleague, friend, and mentor.

A Spreadsheet but Also a Core Value?

Corporate Application

Is excellence a value that is an inseparable part of your organizational culture? If so, how do you measure it? Do your employees take pride in doing their best all the time, or do they give the bare minimum to get by? What impact would peak performance have on your business? When one employee faces challenges or difficult times, what would it mean to have a team that invested in one another rather than sacrifice someone for the good of another? Would improving employee work ethic both individually and as a team improve efficiency and productivity? Would this improvement increase employee morale, retention, and customer service? If you want to enhance the culture of excellence in your organization, consider pursuing veteran hiring initiatives and adding new employees for whom excellence and operating in a high performing team comes as second nature.

Veteran Application

Throughout your service, what specific actions have you taken that demonstrate excellence in all you do? How have you sustained a high level of performance while going above and beyond in your daily duties? How did the excellence you pursued affect team performance? Did it have an impact beyond your team, such as in the community surrounding your duty station, whether stateside or overseas? If you were overseas, how did this excellence affect the multicultural environment in which you operated? If you cannot clearly define ways in which you have served with excellence, how will a potential employer do it, and what incentive do they have to hire you instead of any other candidate?

Dave and his team on a Raven mission with a C-5 doing a Presidential support detail, St Petersburg, Russia – 2002

Dave on a Raven mission with a C-17 in Tajikistan – 2002

A Spreadsheet but Also a Core Value?

Dave supporting the Boy Scouts at a local Veterans Memorial – 2004

"Integrity without knowledge is weak and useless, and knowledge without integrity is dangerous and dreadful."

— Samuel Johnson

Chapter 5
Integrity - The Common Thread Woven into the Core Values Tapestry

Every core value has unique and distinctive characteristics that provide meaning not only to those who possess these values but also to all who interact with them. As unique as each value is, they share a degree of commonality that collectively defines them as "core" values. If one core value were to be defined as the value that weaves all others together, it likely would be integrity. Values such as teamwork, loyalty, selfless service, honor, and excellence would be nearly impossible to possess without a firm and clearly defined base of integrity. For Bob Nunnally, integrity was the foundation and cornerstone upon which he built his twenty-three year career in the US Air Force. It is also the value that has helped him build a highly successful career in the private sector.

A 1980 graduate of the University of Georgia, Bob entered the service on active duty in 1981. Upon receiving his commission as an Air Force officer, he began the long and arduous training process to become a fighter pilot, specifically an F-16 pilot, with later experience in the A-10. Bob became what is known as a Command Pilot, accruing more than two thousand flight hours and flying on dozens of combat missions. A veteran of numerous overseas deployments, he served in Desert Storm and led large NATO forces over Bosnia as well as peacekeeping missions in Europe and the Middle East. Adding to his undergraduate degrees in psychology and history, Bob earned a master's degree in Aeronautical Sciences from Embry-Riddle Aeronautical University and is a graduate of Air Command and Staff College as well as Air War College. His professional development in the Air Force included board president training in safety, controller training in finance, legislative training on Capitol Hill, and even counseling training through social services. Additionally, Bob brings extensive experience in leadership at all levels of an organization as well as diverse multicultural expertise in international settings. As an Air Force officer, he led diverse operations in more than forty countries.

Since retiring from the Air Force in 2004, he has held several roles in leadership and executive consulting; done extensive public speaking and coaching for both large and small organizations, specializing in cultural change; and is an entertaining yet powerfully effective motivational speaker. For several years he ran a successful social media company that he also founded. Today he is a senior executive for a mid-size strategy and IT consulting firm based near Washington, DC.

Civilians often misperceive life in the military, especially that of fighter pilot. Stereotypes are built on popular fighter pilot movies such as *Iron Eagle*, *Independence Day*, and *Top Gun*. Spending time with Bob, however, one easily can see the experiences he cherishes the most are focused around people, not airplanes.

While serving during a very unique time in US history - the Cold War of the 1980s through the multiple combat-deployment times of the early 2000s - he was influenced by those who had lived through the very difficult era of Vietnam; he later put his experience to the test when he led wartime missions in both the Middle East and Eastern Europe. It was in the midst of these cultural changes and generational differences in the military that he had both the opportunity and privilege to mentor and develop new breeds of leaders, many of whom have gone on to serve as top leaders in today's Air Force. These "people development missions" mean the most to him. During his

Thread Woven into the Core Values Tapestry

service, he assembled a band of brothers and sisters he still helps guide and seeks guidance from today.

A telling characteristic of great leaders is not what they have accomplished for themselves but what they have invested in others. Superb leaders are often surrounded by fantastic teams who sense the leader is there to do all he or she can to serve them and help them achieve their best every day. True to the values that made him successful, Bob says his greatest accomplishment had nothing to do with him and everything to do with developing others. He is humble when he talks about his contributions to the careers of others; when one considers the number of people he has led who have gone on to achieve or exceed their leadership and promotion goals, his impact is nothing short of spectacular. More than a dozen individuals he led have earned the rank of Chief Master Sergeant (the top enlisted rank in the Air Force); another dozen plus have earned the rank of Colonel, Brigadier General, or higher. If you ask any of Bob's mentees what he expects of them, the answer is consistent: "Pass it along." In a world where many leaders are simply concerned with their own careers and what's in it for them, this track record speaks volumes to the values by which Bob lives and the character he brings to all he does.

The military has leadership selection and promotion down to a science, as they should, with more than two hundred years of experience in selecting and developing leaders at all levels. Part of the process includes hitting certain benchmarks of training and development along the way. Some call it "checking off the boxes"; in reality, however, it is the minimum level of preparation everyone must have even to be considered for responsibilities commensurate with the next higher pay grade. Bob hit all these benchmarks and along the way took on as many new challenges as he could, always seeking to prepare for the next level. This combination of constantly learning more, exceeding the standards that were expected of him, and taking the time to invest in his development enabled him to be promoted consistently at or below the zone (early) for which he was eligible. He put in long hours and gave selflessly to earn every step he took; he was on a fast track that would take him as high and as far as he desired. Bob's Air Force future was unlimited.

Every goal one sets requires a measure of dedication and sacrifice to achieve the desired success. The loftier the goal, the deeper the measure of sacrifice required. When one is on the journey toward success, it can be easy to get so narrowly focused on attaining a specific achievement that supporting goals and missions become overlooked. A fighter pilot calls this tunnel vision or being "padlocked" on a target, meaning one's preoccupation with hitting the target is so intense that the person loses all sense of his or her surroundings, leaving him or her vulnerable to attack from enemy aircraft and various other hazards. While success often requires pilots to pay a very high price, they can't be so focused that they wind up sacrificing more than needed to achieve the desired result. If they are not vigilant against this, even the best pilots can fall victim to tunnel vision, and in so doing, lose sight of the world around them. Even those with impeccable values and nothing but the best intentions can develop tunnel vision on their way to achieving the success they desire. Bob's tunnel vision came not in the cockpit, but on the way to achieving his belief of what career success and achievement looked like for him. Overcoming his tunnel vision required the use of all his values, especially his integrity.

Integrity can take many forms, and one can define it in many ways. For Bob, and those he mentors and leads, it is defined as doing the right thing, regardless of possible consequences to oneself. To correct his tunnel vision, Bob needed to look into the mirror and see the pending hazards ahead and act in the right way, regardless of the consequences.

As is the case in many career fields outside the military, the better one does in the Air Force the more development opportunities they receive. Many times these opportunities come in the form of educational development limited to a select few. In 1998, Bob received a performance report with a recommendation from his boss (a four-star General) for a definite promotion from Lieutenant Colonel to Colonel, ahead of the promotion cycle he was in. He also had been selected to attend Senior Developmental Education at Harvard, an opportunity afforded to only the best. He had worked his entire career for these opportunities, and they were finally happening. The Air Force was telling him he was among the best of the best.

Thread Woven into the Core Values Tapestry

At a time when he should have been the happiest, however, something didn't sit right with him. After seeking the counsel of his family and his closest mentors, Bob had his answer: tunnel vision. He had done everything right in his career but had lost sight of the hazards of not caring for his family in the ways he should and really wanted. While his family hadn't "crashed and burned" - to use the fighter pilot vernacular - he clearly recognized his commitment to them wasn't the same as it was to the Air Force. He had a substantial imbalance between work and family; he had spent long hours at the office, missed important family events, and skipped vacation altogether. After painstaking consideration, Bob knew he faced a critical decision: should he continue on the same path for the fulfillment he desired, or take a step back and work to put things into proper balance? When he turned to his core values, integrity called him to fulfill his commitments and uphold his ethical beliefs, regardless of the consequences he might face.

Bob realized that staying on the path he was on only would lead to a greater imbalance between work and family. His tunnel vision would grow stronger, and the cost of success would continue to increase. In the end he knew the price required for success would be greater than he was willing to pay. For things to change, he had to change his direction, so he did just that. After he made his decision, he went to his boss (the four-star General) to have one of the more difficult conversations he has ever had. He asked his boss to withdraw his recommendation for early promotion and give his seat at Harvard to someone else. Bob knew it was the right thing to do, but he was concerned about the fallout and potential repercussions of his decision. In essence he was ending his career progression, and once his boss withdrew his recommendation, he could not change course. This was a once in a lifetime chance, with no opportunity for a do-over. While he knew it was the right thing to do, what would his boss, his peers, and his team think of him? How would the Air Force system react?

Braced for the worst, he was surprised by the reaction that came once word of his decision got out. Instead of anger, resentment, or disappointment, he found compassion, respect, and understanding. Rather than being shunned, he was embraced, and the discussions he had as a result helped him grow as a person and helped him know he had made the right decision. Bob's commitment to his values ultimately provided him a true opportunity to succeed at one of the most important things in life: balance.

Unfortunately, since transitioning into life in the private sector, Bob has found that not everyone shares the same values he learned in the Air Force, especially his commitment to integrity. Regardless of the values others hold, he remains true to the ones he has lived by for decades. Unequivocally he knows holding true to his integrity has provided him with great success, as he has achieved or exceeded every goal he has set for himself since leaving the Air Force.

Recently, Bob stepped into a role that carried great risk. A key client with a $25 million account was unhappy with his company. The contract would soon be up for renewal, and the client was considering other vendors. Because of work pressures and leadership changes, many of the employees serving the client felt confused and underappreciated, which resulted in a very unhappy client. Understandably, the client was uncertain about the company's commitment to them. Bob took on the unenviable task of repairing the relationship so the company would not lose this important account.

Bob put his own integrity on the line and worked to clean up the relationship. By holding true to his word and delivering on all commitments, he was able to refocus and reinvigorate the team. Daily meetings with the client helped communicate actions and detail the exact promises upon which the company would deliver. When the team underperformed, Bob said so, knowing that integrity means doing what is right, regardless of the consequences. Bob took the extra step to explain why the company had faltered, and more important, how it would better serve the client. Just as he had throughout his Air Force career, he demonstrated integrity to both his team and to his customer. His team followed his lead, showing their commitment to integrity both to him and the client. In the end, Bob and his team were able to convert a $25 million jeopardy account into a $50 million non-jeopardy account. The account would not have been saved, let alone double in size, without an integrity that built a firm foundation and a solid footing for future growth.

Thread Woven into the Core Values Tapestry

Some people might say that Bob has been lucky over the course of his career both in and out of the military. This is only true if luck is defined as the place where preparation and opportunity meet. Bob has taken every step along the way to prepare himself to be ready when opportunities come his way. Most of the people he served with followed the same recipe for success as he did. Aside from integrity, two specific values he believes most military personnel bring to the private sector are teamwork and problem solving. While there may be many keys to success in finding and hiring the right veterans for the right roles in a company, understanding the power of these two values is near the top of Bob's list for leveraging the success of veterans.

The nature of daily work in the military epitomizes loyalty and working together in a team environment to accomplish goals that require abilities that are greater than the skills of any one individual. While this is precisely what corporate America seeks, it poses great challenges both to veterans interviewing for employment opportunities and for those in the hiring process who have difficulty translating the true worth of their experience.

Veterans do nearly everything in a team environment; when asked what they personally accomplished, they often have difficulty separating the success of the team from their own contributions. Ironically the same integrity that holds a team together also can prevent many veterans from achieving the level of personal success they envision when leaving the military. While veterans must clearly define and communicate the success they helped their teams achieve, potential employers must understand the return on investment of helping veterans explain not simply individual success, but how deeply they are committed to contributing in a team environment. Employers should use the popular interview technique called "peeling the onion" to cut deeply enough to get to the true worth any candidate brings, especially when interviewing veterans.

While military service mirrors much of what happens in life outside the military, the challenges service members overcome daily can be far more complicated and often involve matters of life and death. The differences do not stop at the intensity of the problems faced but continue with other factors. Most notable is the ability to quickly solve the problem at hand and achieve the most successful outcome possible. When these problems occur, however, they are usually not symmetric and do not have simple, safe solutions that can be found in a manual.

The problems military personnel face are often unique and complicated, and if not handled appropriately, very bad things can and do happen. This is further complicated by the location in which the problem occurs, as cultural differences can play a key role in defining the problem's solution and often severely limit the available options. From the most junior personnel to the most experienced leader, all are trained to solve complex, ever-changing problems as quickly and safely as possible. Solutions are formed, altered, and implemented in real time with real consequences; time and again, military members deliver and provide success for both the team and each individual involved. Failure is not an option; the problem must be solved. There is no finer training ground for ethically solving problems than service in the US military. When others see no solution to real-world problems, military personnel understand the implications of failure and call on all resources at their disposal to achieve success.

For thirty years, Bob has proven his worth both in the military and the private sector. While the transition was not easy, he has used all the values he learned from the beginning of his career until now and has become more successful than even he could have envisioned. He has worked hard and been rewarded for his efforts, but he gives the bulk of the credit for his success to the firm foundation his mentors helped him build - one based on unwavering integrity and a faith in teamwork and problem solving. He seeks to pass these values along and demands them every day from his team.

While there is only one Bob Nunnally in this world, the good news is there are millions of veterans like him who possess the same skills and track record of success and who are ready to provide great value for a broad range of companies.

Thread Woven into the Core Values Tapestry

Corporate Application

Has your company clearly defined the values it upholds? Do these values define the culture of the company, or is there a gap between values and culture? Do your employees understand how values build culture, and are they aligned with those values? Is integrity the cornerstone upon which all other values and the company culture is built? Does leadership respect these values, and would they handle a career changing decision similar to Bob's in the same way his boss did? Does your company have the internal resources to properly define, identify, and attract the right veterans for positions you are seeking to fill? Would your company culture and dynamic change if you hired veterans skilled in teamwork and adept at problem solving? If the current picture of your organization does not match the desired picture, what is your plan to change this, and how could veteran hiring elicit these changes?

Veteran Application

How do you define your experience around core values? What decisions have you made that were extremely difficult and had at least two options from which to choose but only one path that should be followed based on your values? How did integrity play out in your decision making processes, and what implications might have arisen if you had gone against your values and chosen a different path? Defining clear examples of how these values and choices have led to positive results is critical to success in any interview and hiring process. Regardless of the position for which you are being considered, *all* companies need people with integrity to join their team. The better you, as a candidate, demonstrate examples of integrity, teamwork, and problem solving, the easier your transition will be.

Major Bob Nunnally prior to a flight in his F-16

Thread Woven into the Core Values Tapestry

2012

"Only those who have learned the power of sincere and selfless contribution experience life's deepest joy: true fulfillment."

- Tony Robbins

Chapter 6
The Journey from Selfish to Selfless Service

Most people who serve in the military do so to fulfill a desire to accomplish something bigger than themselves; they are truly interested in and feel called to service. That said, it often takes years to truly understand what selfless service means and how one can practically achieve it in all he or she does. The journey from selfish to selfless happens over time and with repeated sacrifices, which builds a maturity that only comes with significant life experience, regardless of a person's age or status in life. A military career can be thrilling and provide memorable adrenalin rushes one never will forget. Ask veterans what has been their most memorable career accomplishment, though, and the answers usually will have little to do with the adrenalin rush and quickly turn to selfless service and helping others. Such is the case with Jeff Imsdahl.

Jeff is a native of St. Paul, Minnesota, and except for the two years he spent during his childhood in California, he grew up in the northern outskirts of the Twin Cities metro area. His childhood is not dissimilar to that of many others; his mother divorced when he was young and remarried a couple of years later. His step-dad quickly filled the role of father, role model, and hero. Jeff is the oldest of three children and spent his youth excelling in sports of all kinds before graduating from Forest Lake High School in 1986. He headed to Winona State University on a football scholarship and soon found he enjoyed it more than academics. As his grades were not sufficient for him to keep the scholarship, both his football career and status as a full-time college student ended after just one year.

His father, Terry, had served as a Military Policeman during Vietnam, and Jeff had a great deal of respect for those who served in the military. He explored options in the Army and was set to take the next steps with them; he had invited the recruiter to his home so he could make a commitment to the Army. Whether by chance or providence, the Army recruiter had trouble finding Main Street in the small town where Jeff lived and never showed up. His father suggested maybe it was a sign he should consider other options, such as the Air Force or Navy. Jeff eventually made his way to an Air Force recruiter and discussed his interest in law enforcement. The recruiter showed him a few videos of missions a security specialist would complete in the woods, on convoys, and in a variety of other roles; Jeff was hooked and left for basic training at the end of January 1988.

Early in his career, Jeff had the opportunity to gain valuable experience in leadership and diversity that he did not learn growing up in Minnesota. Living north of the Twin Cities in the 1980s did not provide much experience regarding diversity. Military culture, however, did and also taught him how effective team management is implemented, regardless of where fellow team members come from or look like. While Jeff previously struggled with the rigors of academia, he thrived in various military schools that taught him skills he still uses to this day, both in and out of the military. Initially Jeff specialized in nuclear security and was selected to attend one of the most difficult security schools the Air Force offered, which carried a washout rate of more than 25 percent, the Ground-Launched Cruise Missile course. He excelled at the school and earned distinguished graduate status and was ranked fifth out of 110 students.

Over the years, Jeff's career has taken him to Europe, South America, and the Middle East, where he has supported Security Forces missions in

The Journey from Selfish to Selfless Service

Operations JUST CAUSE, DESERT SHIELD, DESERT STORM, PROVIDE COMFORT, NOBLE COMFORT and IRAQI FREEDOM. In 1996 Jeff left active duty to continue his career in the Air Force Reserve. In 2012 he was promoted to the rank of Chief Master Sergeant, the highest enlisted pay grade in the Air Force. He currently serves as the Security Forces Manager for the 934th Airlift Wing in Minneapolis, where he advises his commander on all matters concerning the health, welfare, morale, and effective management of more than 160 enlisted members. His chief responsibility is taking care of the team and ensuring leadership does everything they can to meet this objective.

Jeff is the epitome of "not your average Joe" and the values that come with service, but it is something he has grown into; he joined the service as we all do, as an average Joe. When he began as a young Airman, he was there to learn a skill as a part of his service. As he grew in rank and responsibility, his role and mission began to grow into something far different; he became a teacher, a mentor, and a role model responsible for guiding the next generation of Security Forces personnel. His character was forged by veterans who had honed their skills in Vietnam during an era of service when the draft had mandated service of the masses. Jeff learned a great deal from those who remained and had built successful military careers post Vietnam. Long before "service before self" was an official Air Force core value, these senior enlisted leaders taught Jeff why it mattered. He learned that if he focused on the betterment of the Air Force, his unit, and the lives of others he protected, his own needs would be taken care of in the process. A focus solely on his goals would be of little value if he accomplished everything he set his mind to while his team constantly failed. Selfless service for him means taking care of the "whole" first while letting the "self" follow. His leaders did not just teach him that this was important; they showed him. He saw it every day, whether he was walking a post or manning a desk.

When Jeff speaks of his accomplishments, his humble nature is quickly evident. Beyond the military, Jeff is proud to be a father. As a divorced father who shared custody of his two sons, he had many demands on his time. Jeff, however, does not consider the time he spent with his boys a sacrifice but rather his duty as a father. He remained close enough to them that he could help with coaching their sports teams, attend band concerts, and show up for the everyday life events that every father should commit to being a part of. Regardless of the divorce, his selfless commitment to his children remained, and he has managed to show them how to hold true to their responsibilities. This is not only a valuable lesson for his children; every chance he gets, as a senior enlisted leader in the Air Force, he passes this value on to the newest generations of those who choose military service.

Professionally, Jeff has achieved many things in the military, not the least of which is holding the highest enlisted rank in the Air Force. Less than one percent of the force will reach this level; it is a true testament to who Jeff is and, more important, who he has become. His most precious accomplishment, however, happened during his time in Kirkuk, Iraq. In support of Operation IRAQI FREEDOM he deployed with more than thirty of his own Security Forces personnel from Minneapolis. He assumed a leadership role responsible for more than seventy personnel who provided force protection services at one of the busiest and most dangerous air bases in Iraq. His team deployed to Iraq from bases around the world, not just US Air Force bases but a blended team of forces from a number of coalition nations supporting the mission in Iraq. They were there for at least six months at a time. The team members spoke different languages and came from different cultures while operating in a deadly environment with a unique culture all its own, yet they all shared the same mission. Suddenly those years of service and life lessons in diversity, team development, and performance were never more important for Jeff as he assumed this challenging new role. While the team was tested repeatedly, they did what all successful teams do, they stood strong. They secured the sectors they were responsible for without a single team member being killed or wounded in action. For Jeff, no award or decoration could be pinned on his chest that would be remotely as valuable as knowing that all of his people executed their mission and returned home safely. This truly is selfless service, taking care of the "whole" first while letting the "self" follow.

Jeff lives a life with no regrets; his experiences have shaped him and allow him to shape others in ways that may take them down a smoother path

The Journey from Selfish to Selfless Service

than the one he has traveled. One disappointment that does stand out for him is his lack of performance when he was given the chance to complete his education and play football at Winona State. As he looks back, he believes that if he stayed on that path he likely would not have served his country in the Air Force. He does not regret changing paths but rather is disappointed in his own poor performance, which led him to the change in direction. Jeff also knows that opportunities like the one he had to earn a free education are limited, and he wishes he had taken advantage of it when he was there. He has been successful despite his incomplete education and seeks to finish what he started long ago. He is one class shy of his Community College of the Air Force associate degree and currently is enrolled in a criminal justice program to complete his bachelor's degree; he has approximately five classes remaining. While the degree will be of little value professionally at this point in his career, he understands that to lead and enforce standards for others he also must meet those same standards. This is yet another example of taking care of the "whole" first while letting the "self" follow by setting a positive example and meeting or exceeding the standards in his own life, regardless of the value it brings back to him.

Jeff has directly applied the values he has learned in the military to his life in the private sector. Working for a Fortune 300 utilities provider, he leads a team that protects vital utility resources that provide service to millions of customers nationwide. While his job is to lead a team that secures facilities, he considers it much more than that. Just as Jeff's team did in Iraq, his company doesn't just secure assets; it secures people. Without these people, the mission of providing utilities nationwide never could be accomplished. He also seeks to find ways to go above and beyond in all his team does. At one point, metal theft at remote facilities was an escalating problem that cost the company money as well as resources to deal with service interruptions; it also opened the company to safety liabilities for their own employees and the thieves who were stealing the metal. Many in his position would not bother trying to solve this problem; it was beyond the scope of what defined success in his role and was simply a cost of doing business. Jeff knew better, though. Resources spent on this issue were resources the company could more effectively allocate if the problem was solved. He tackled the issue head on and has spent countless hours taking his team above and beyond to lower theft rates and create a safer environment for all employees. Fewer service outages translate into higher customer satisfaction rates and greater job security for everyone on his team. Doing the right thing for the team has led to greater security for all.

Jeff sees many correlations between military service and success in the private sector, which he believes all employers should clearly understand. Military service forges values that are difficult to cultivate in almost any other environment, certainly not in the same condensed timeframe the military teaches them. Additionally, many with military service may not yet have earned a diploma, but the experiences and skills they bring to any employer cannot be learned in any diploma program. Formal education should be valued, but so should life education taught through military service. These life experiences include working in close quarters where the team is more important than the individual. These teams operate around the world and require cultural awareness, sensitivity, and a commitment to diversity that doesn't just check off boxes regarding team composition but rather has the right people in place to do the right job at every moment. Selfless service also shapes a work ethic that sacrifices for the good of all. Whether a service member stands post in Iraq or supports a daily mission stateside, the challenges don't end based on the position of the hands on the clock. Great leaders understand this and know how to maximize performance by taking advantage of lulls in the work tempo to reward team members with time away when they can take it. Jeff's whole philosophy really is summed up with "Focus on the 'whole' first while letting the 'self' follow."

In the military we use the term "force multiplier," which is something that is used to enhance strength and increase it to a level it could not be without the enhancement. A good example of this is a military working dog. When two Security Forces members respond to a disturbance call with a sizable crowd gathering in protest on the perimeter of the base, they are vastly outnumbered and the situation quickly can escalate. It is not practical and in most cases reasonable to match person for person the number of personnel responding to the number of protestors. So how do you multiply the

The Journey from Selfish to Selfless Service

force to create the appearance of a much larger force capable of handling the protestors should they decide to escalate? Send a military working dog with the response team. The mere presence of the dog will act as a multiplier to increase the perceived size and ability of the force. Two members turn into the power of ten or twenty. On a cold winter's day, add a fire hose to the same scenario, and suddenly two personnel, a dog, and a fire hose can handle a substantial crowd. So it is with mentoring and professional development. It is not always possible or practical to give specific and tailored mentorship and professional development on an individual basis. Nor can each mentor provide all the information and training one individual needs to develop properly. A force multiplier is needed to increase the ratio of members being developed to the mentors available. The power of one person to mentor many on his or her team helps lift the team to new heights and shape a dynamic culture that focuses on serving others. As changes occur in the team's personnel, the culture remains embedded with the remaining team members and spreads to the new members on the team. Those who leave the team carry the culture with them and share it with others. Hence, the work of one effective mentor is a force multiplier that can reach dozens of team members without any direct contact with them whatsoever.

Jeff's mentors were force multipliers, and in turn he has become one too. I know this because when I began my time in the Air Force I did so as a junior enlisted member in a Security Forces Squadron, the same Squadron in which Jeff was serving as a Master Sergeant (E-7) and still serves in today. He was one of the first people I met, and I was fortunate to have several interactions with him during my time there, which I will never forget. He was my force multiplier, teaching me valuable skills that I have passed on to others I've mentored in the nine years since I served with him. Even as I was selected to receive my commission and to be promoted to a position senior to Jeff's, the mentoring did not end. While others might let pride get in the way of the team and have me figure things out on my own, Jeff was always there to answer the call should I need help. He knew from experience that the more he could teach me and others the stronger the Air Force team would be, and these strengths would be carried on long after he was gone. He remains a true friend and mentor. Regardless of where our careers take us, we know we always can count on each other to mentor others in selfless service.

Corporate Application

Does your company have a culture that develops selfless service and encourages mentorship at all levels? Is this mentorship intentional, or is it left to a series of chance encounters that may never happen? Does top leadership drive this cultural development, and do they put selflessness on display for all to see? Are team members valued more for the diverse experiences they bring to the fight or for where they come from and the schools they attended? If you cannot clearly define your culture the way it is defined in this chapter, consider adding seasoned veterans at all levels in your organization and take the journey from a culture of selfish to selfless service.

Veteran Application

Which of your experiences clearly define selfless service? What situations have you been in that required selfless actions, and what results were delivered due to your specific actions? How did these results affect the team as a whole? What diverse work environments have you been a part of or led during your time in the military? How was the mission more successful as a result of the team's diversity, and can you clearly define this increased productivity for a potential employer? All kinds of companies need employees who can thrive in a diverse team environment. If you cannot translate the value you bring in this regard, how do you expect a potential employer to translate it for you, and why should they be interested in hiring you? Since 2001 many service members have deployed overseas, not just to fight in a war but also operate in small diverse teams in austere locations and be immersed in cultures that were foreign to them. If this describes you, learn to tell the story of how you succeeded under those conditions. If you can achieve success in those environments, your success story can translate to success in any environment.

Jeff talking to troops in Iraq

"The supreme quality for leadership is unquestionably integrity. Without it, no real success is possible, no matter whether it is on a section gang, a football field, in an army, or in an office."

- Pres. Dwight D. Eisenhower

Chapter 7
Programming Your Moral Code—Integrity

Whether due to the demand to fill a never ending news cycle or a true lack of values in the market, there seems to be a steady stream of new financial scandals reported almost daily. From manipulative accounting practices to building a financial house of cards that collapses in on itself or forcing the sale of needless products and services to earn more commissions, these events appear to happen more and more frequently. One would think only those of little moral character would choose a profession in accounting or financial services. After all, when was the last time a news flash was broadcast that trumpeted the financial planner who called a client and said a financial mistake had been made in the firm's favor and insisted on refunding the difference to the client? While it may never be reported, it does happen; a Marine who enlisted twenty years ago applies the same values he learned to defend his country as he does to defend his customers and his business.

Like so many others, Tom began his time in the US Marine Corps looking for direction and a purpose. He was enrolled in college and wandering somewhat aimlessly through classes that failed to hold his interest. During Christmas break in 1992, he decided to speak with a Marine recruiter. In short order the recruiter helped him find the purpose he was looking for. Tom chose the Military Police as his career field and was in basic training a few short weeks later in February 1993. He served as a reservist, so his career was less eventful in the way of deployments than those who have served since 2001, but his experiences have not been any less meaningful. In the summers, Tom spent time doing annual training at Twentynine Palms in the California desert, no easy task during the heat of the summer. He participated in multiple Toys for Tots campaigns in Minneapolis and was activated to help with devastation caused by the flooding of the Red River on the border of Minnesota and North Dakota near Grand Forks in 1997. After completing his initial enlistment, he received an honorable discharge in 1999.

Tom learned many lessons during his time in the Marine Corps and considers them some of the most valuable developmental years of his life. He maintains several lifelong friendships with others he met while serving, and he values the bonds that have remained tight throughout the years. Although he wasn't called to active duty, he enjoyed training and preparing for missions should the need arise. The teamwork and service to others through toy drives and flood response gave him the purpose he was looking for in a life mission greater than him. His training built discipline, and this disciplined repetition increased his preparedness not only to go to battle but also for any other tasks he would undertake. Tom learned he was capable of performing at a very high level, and as situations changed, he was capable of adjusting his efforts to achieve the same outstanding performance. Service in any branch brings a sense of accomplishment; completing training and doing a tour of duty in the Marine Corps carries a special pride, as you know you are one of "the few, the proud." Tom knew if he could make it through everything the Marines could throw at him he could make it through anything. Throughout the years he has proven this time and again. He returned to college after completing his initial military training and finished a degree in youth ministry at Bethel University in 1996. He also balanced military service and school with two years of playing football at Bethel.

While anyone who knows Tom would say he most certainly possesses the confidence to be successful in any endeavor he pursues, his humble nature is clearly evident. Although his list of accomplishments is long and includes serving in the Marines, completing college, and playing football, he says that

Programming Your Moral Code—Integrity

serving his family as a husband and father and building a business from nothing are his greatest accomplishments. Tom is most impressed not with what he has done but rather who he has become as a person, the result of values taught through solid family examples and a strong faith in Christ and later forged in him during his service as a Marine. Without these values, he clearly understands he would not be where he is today and just how blessed he has been.

Professionally, Tom translated the values and discipline he learned in the military to build a successful business as a financial advisor. He began in 2000 with a dozen other new advisors seeking to live the American dream and build their own successful businesses. By 2008 he was the last of them left in the industry. The financial markets have seen numerous steep declines and since 2000 have basically been flat. Yet during the same challenging times, Tom has built a business from no assets in management to more than $150 million and from no clients to more than three hundred. He has climbed from a rookie to ranking in the top 25 percent of all advisors companywide and continues to climb in the rankings. He gives credit to the discipline he learned in the Marines for his being able to conceive a vision when others could not and formulating a plan and staying with it regardless of how difficult the course was. While Tom understands the importance of discipline, his most cherished value is integrity, and he has built a successful business with this value as his cornerstone.

As is the case with many veterans, Tom has learned through the years that those around him do not always share the values he holds as fundamental to success in any environment. The lack of integrity and moral fiber on the part of many has disappointed him. His greatest disappointment, however, has resulted in perhaps his greatest professional success and put his values and integrity on the line for all to see.

Tom built a book of business early in his career and got to a point where he was ready to take on more. Through a relationship with another advisor, he came to an agreement to merge the two businesses into one. He would manage both books of business, and the other advisor would eventually phase out of the business altogether. On the surface all seemed to be healthy; assets appeared well allocated and properly balanced between risk and reward. After the agreement was finalized, however, the market changed dramatically; what seemed well balanced previously began to spiral out of control rapidly. The portfolio Tom had assumed and agreed to compensate the other advisor for was suddenly down dramatically, in part due to market conditions but also structural issues with asset allocation. The book of business that was represented was vastly overinflated against the way it would actually perform. So what did Tom do? He held strong with unquestionable integrity and honored the agreement he had made. He began the tedious and painful work of meeting with clients and being honest with them about the situation and which options were available, including taking their accounts elsewhere should they desire to do so. Instinct would tell us that most would leave; their portfolios were in tatters, and whether or not Tom was responsible for it was inconsequential. To Tom's surprise, most of the clients did not leave. Because he was honest with them and gave them options, he was able to repair the damage; he retained an astonishing 80 percent of those clients. Ask Tom why they stayed, and his response is one word, "Integrity."

A classic definition of integrity is always doing the right thing even when no one is looking. Why does someone do the right thing if no one is looking? Shouldn't there be more to it than that? Tom gives valuable insight regarding why he does the right thing regardless of who is looking. For him, integrity is the moral code that guides him. Look at any piece of electronic equipment today. Its inner workings are programmed with codes that direct its behavior. While codes can be modified or changed, they cannot change the response of the equipment without the equipment being reprogrammed. Codes can be changed quickly, but reprogramming takes time. Furthermore, not everyone is capable of even modifying the code, let alone reprogramming it. Such is the case with human behavior. Tom's military service programmed "values codes" into him that cannot be changed to fit the situation he is in. Tom has integrity regarding even the small things and knows it will be there in equal proportion during more difficult times as well. It is in his moral code, and once programmed it is very difficult to change. For him the Marine Corps was the single best place for him to develop these values and program his moral code to guide him through the rest of his life. This has allowed him

Programming Your Moral Code—Integrity

to do things the right way, whether or not clients always know it, and leaves him with no regrets. Has it worked? The growth of his business over more than a decade of turbulent markets says it has. He has not only survived but also thrived.

Beyond his values, two things make Tom an outstanding financial advisor; his ability to see the big picture in the market and also take actions in the best interest of his clients to keep them on the path toward long-term success. He resists making changes to a portfolio simply because there is money in it; not making the changes would result in not realizing additional profit, what some consider "free money." Customers come first, and the more success they have, the better he will do over the long term. His customers know this. It is a key reason they stay with him and why referrals are his largest source of new business; he does no advertising. Recently he had a client who, through a paperwork error, was charged for two extra trades. The trades were needless and unintentional on Tom's part and did not really harm the client, except the client was charged additional commissions for these trades. With the volume on the account, there is no conceivable way the client would have known what had happened, that is, until Tom revealed the error. He let the client know he would make it right and reverse the commissions; in the short term this did not have much impact on either of them. Over the long term, though, this simple act of honesty and integrity solidified the client/advisor relationship and took what was already strong and made it considerably stronger. The client knows Tom delivers good results and that they can trust him with the assets they put under his care.

Tom's preparation for a career in financial services began long before he started working for his current company. In the Marine Corps, he trained and prepared for every situation he could. However, when outside factors were applied to the situation he found himself in, the result often would be something that looked dramatically different than what he originally had anticipated. In the military, this is referred to as being in the "fog of war"; when the bullets start to fly, even the best-laid plans are modified to adapt to the current situation on the ground. This mirrors closely the life of any professional in financial services. Tom cannot plan for everything, but he can prepare himself and his clients to weather any storms that come their way so that they pull through with minimal, if any, damage done. Since 2000 the market has been erratic at best, and predicting which way it will go can be maddening. When working with clients, Tom knows to prepare both himself and them for whatever may arise. Integrity plays a vital role in the preparation and execution of everything he does each day.

Tom shares sage advice not only for employers looking at why they should consider hiring more veterans but also for veterans who do not understand how to properly communicate the value they bring to any future employer. Not all employees are programmed with the same moral code; values such as work ethic and integrity are sometimes of little importance. If these values are important to your organization, know that veterans tend to share these as a common part of their core and is a compelling reason why they should be considered for employment. Veterans come from a culture in which failure is not an option under almost any circumstance. Understanding this and the tireless dedication they bring to nearly any task will add great value to veteran hiring initiatives. If you are a veteran, clearly define how you have lived these values and, more important, how they have made you successful in everything you do.

Tom is a proud yet humble veteran of the US Marine Corps. He is forever indebted to the Corps for the values they forged in him during his service. As someone who has known Tom for nearly twenty years, I am proud to have called him teammate (in football), fellow alum (at Bethel), colleague (in military service), and my financial advisor. Few are blessed with better friends than Tom, and for this reason I am most proud to call him, above all other titles, my friend.

Corporate Application

What moral code does your company follow? Have you had employee relations issues in the past (or currently) that are a direct result of poor programming of the moral code? How does this affect your company culture as a whole? How does it affect employee satisfaction and retention? More important, how does it impact the business you do outside of your four walls

Programming Your Moral Code—Integrity

every day with clients? Does your company have time to reprogram those who come with faulty moral coding? If not, what are you doing to emphasize a better values-based fit for all potential new employees? Do you have specific veteran hiring initiatives aimed at capturing the best from this group and reshaping a culture that needs an updated moral code with key values such as integrity? If not, why? If preparation is the key to success, what are you doing to prepare for the unknown while shaping a culture that will adapt without compromising values?

Veteran Application

Just as Tom defined integrity by giving specific examples of how using his moral code has resulted in success, how have you succeeded in your career while displaying integrity? Integrity is not situational; there are no small lapses with integrity. One either has it or not. What seems small to you may well be exactly the situation that a potential employer is looking to improve. Be prepared to give clear and concise examples of how you have lived with integrity and other core values; clearly defining the value you bring will lead to greater interview success. Never underestimate the power of values, the depth at which you possess them, and the impact they will have with the right employer.

Tom and his family after graduation from basic training – 1993

Programming Your Moral Code—Integrity

Tom during field training – 1993

"We gain strength, and courage, and confidence by each experience in which we really stop to look fear in the face.... We must do that which we think we cannot."

- Eleanor Roosevelt

Chapter 8
Strength – The Bond That Holds a Team Together

The strength of any team lies not just in the skills they possess but also their ability to persist through adversity and press on to achieve the goals of the mission with which they were tasked. Even the most seasoned teams experience adversity at some point on their journeys, but their success lies in their response to the challenging circumstances they face. The same is true not just in a team environment but also with each individual effort put forth, efforts that contribute to the collective efforts of the team. Military history is full of stories of those who have achieved great things both as individuals and as part of a team, all the while overcoming every obstacle placed in their way. I found just such a story of strength and persistence through adversity in Andrea Bond.

A native of Minnesota, Andrea enlisted in the US Army at age seventeen. After completing basic and advanced training, she joined the 682nd Engineer Battalion in the Minnesota Army National Guard. When one is seventeen, the military is a tough adventure, even more so when the individual is in an administrative role as the first and only female in the unit for her first year and a half. For Andrea this was a very early lesson about strength and working through challenging times when she felt all alone. Outside of her Army service, she was attending college and studying law enforcement before switching paths and pursuing aviation. She earned a bachelor's degree in Aviation from Minnesota State University, Mankato. After graduating she put a packet in for consideration with the aviation board and was selected for the Minnesota Army National Guard Officer Candidate School (OCS) program to receive her commission as a 2nd Lieutenant with a follow on flight school assignment in Alabama.

Andrea faced more challenges during her time in OCS when her brother was tragically killed halfway through the course. She was devastated and brokenhearted. Everything in her told her to quit; she saw no possible way to continue on and complete OCS. As she contemplated her future in the program, she felt the power of strength and persistence in a very different way – through her team of fellow officer candidates. She quickly learned the importance not only of individual strength in making it through challenging times but also the extraordinary strength a team can bring when they refuse to leave a teammate behind. When a fellow soldier is down and in need of help in hostile territory, the team will gather around him or her to provide 360-degree security. They provide protection for those on the team who may not be able to provide it for themselves; they will not let them quit and will never leave them behind. This is precisely what they did for Andrea. Her fellow officer candidates lifted her up during these painful times and provided her with a blanket of protection until she was able to get back on her feet and join the front lines with the rest of her team. She always will be grateful to her team for this life lesson in strength and never will forget their persistence in keeping her from giving up.

Flight school in any branch of the military is competitive, and the stakes are extremely high; you meet standards or you go home. Pushing students through who fail to meet standards puts the lives of all around them at risk. Andrea was in a very competitive environment, one in which the class size was fifty and she was one of only four females. She was determined, however, to make it through flight school and be rated as a Blackhawk helicopter pilot. She again called on her inner strength and persevered through what would

Strength – The Bond That Holds a Team Together

be a challenging school for any student; in 2004 she was named an honor graduate and ranked in the top 5 percent of her class.

Andrea has held various positions in the last decade, including pilot, executive officer, public affairs staff member, and Company Commander. She also has done community work as a Yellow Ribbon Outreach Coordinator. Early in 2007 she left for training in Oklahoma in preparation for deployment to Iraq as a Blackhawk pilot. She spent a year flying battlefield transport missions throughout Iraq with an average of three missions a week and more than 350 total flying hours. She again called on her strength to safely complete all her missions, but this time things were different. She was a leader; her strength affected others on her crew; and she had to stay strong. Andrea also had a very unique opportunity to help lead the first all-female Blackhawk crew to fly missions in Iraq or any combat theater. Her strength had been built over the years through mentors and teammates who were there for her at every step on her journey; it was now being replicated in others she was leading. Just as with all mentoring, the more you give away, the better you become at whatever skill you are teaching. In this case, the more Andrea gave strength to others, the stronger she became. It is this personnel development that has been a highlight of her career. Andrea returned from Iraq in July 2008 and continues to touch the lives of others wherever she goes.

Andrea's achievements exceed almost all standards by which others judge success. Even with a distinguished list of where she has been and what she has accomplished along the way, she reflects on when she did not always give her very best. As is the case with many people who are driven to succeed, her ambition sometimes has led her to take on more than she should; the result is a juggling act in which one task suffers at the expense of another. While she has the ability to be successful in all she sets her mind to, there have been instances when she could have backed away from voluntary additional responsibilities to maintain balance and ensure that her tasks received the focus and effort they deserved. She has learned that by taking a bit more time to make deliberate and thoughtful decisions she will achieve greater balance and more consistent success. Make no mistake, her performance over the years has been exemplary, but she knows she could have done even better with the right balance and focus.

Andrea's formula for success isn't complicated. She focuses on a whole person concept to remain strong mentally, physically, spiritually, and emotionally. Consider the example of a chair with four legs; when something is out of balance, the integrity of the entire chair can be compromised. So it is with the strength needed to keep various areas of life properly balanced. The more the chair gets out of balance, the easier it becomes to make poor decisions based on subjective emotions rather than objective facts. Andrea's strength defines her character and allows her to persevere through even the greatest of challenges. She understands the value of introspection along with self-critical analysis and self-deprecation when even she can't believe she made such a comical decision. When she is able to laugh at herself, it releases her to focus on her performance in any task rather than worry what others will think of her. She stays true to her values, and the performance follows. Her inner strength, family, and faith in God have shaped her positive attitude and given her a passion for trying new things and risking failure, rather than not trying at all. For some, much of what she has done is out of their comfort zone. Andrea, however, has not lived beyond her comfort zone; rather, she has quietly redefined the boundaries of her comfort zone and along the way grown into a significantly more valuable person than she imagined possible.

Andrea sees a direct correlation between the strength and perseverance she learned in the military and her transition to a career in the private sector. Military service is structured very differently than life in the private sector, specifically as it relates to how an individual finds new employment. At most levels in the military, interviews are not commonplace, and networking specifically for the benefit of your next position is a somewhat foreign concept. Networks are built more by reputation among those with whom you have served; your reputation spreads without much effort, whether it is good or bad. Transitioning beyond military service is often difficult for many veterans. As discussed earlier in this book, while interviewing they usually are comfortable discussing team accomplishments yet often find it difficult to quantify how they contributed specifically to the success of the team. Andrea

Strength – The Bond That Holds a Team Together

has found that the strength she gained in the military is a quality employers seek; while she might feel uncomfortable at first, she can apply the same discipline she learned in the Army to successfully network her way to the right opportunity. She also has learned how to add shape and substance to the values that drive her actions, define her strengths, and bring clarity to the depth of character she possesses. Her ability to focus more on her own performance and less on what others think of her has allowed her to make connections many others would not. "Better to try and fail than not to try at all" is a guiding principle for her.

Andrea has been fortunate to have been involved at the state level with the Yellow Ribbon program, working closely with communities and businesses across the state to bridge the knowledge gap between the military and private sectors. She has seen firsthand the struggles other soldiers go through during times of career transition; she both learns from them and shares resources she has found helpful. Her strength and words of encouragement provide comfort and reinforce the values veterans bring to the workforce; she helps them know they are not alone. Through her public affairs work she has participated in media projects that help define the contributions veterans have made in the military as well as the performance a company can expect when it hires the right veterans. Regardless of the size of the impact, she continues to define value for veterans wherever and whenever she is able.

Time and again Andrea has proven that in the face of adversity she will stand strong. The discipline she has gained over the years has developed her strength and perseverance, which in turn has enhanced her ability to process information quickly and efficiently; she consistently makes accurate and timely decisions regardless of the duress she is under. Chances are better than average that she will never be put in a corporate position where the consequences of failure are greater than or even equal to those of flying a Blackhawk helicopter full of personnel around a foreign battlefield three times a week for a year. She is tried, tested, and true, and her experiences in the military have made her a stronger person. The stronger she is, the stronger the team is and the greater the adversity they can and will overcome together.

Andrea realizes how blessed she is to have received the rewards of growth and professional development in return for the exceptional efforts she has put forth. While there is a uniqueness to her story, there are thousands more out there who have overcome adversity and achieved levels of success they never could have envisioned. One of the ways Andrea seeks to give back is by helping employers in the private sector understand precisely what veterans bring to the workforce. Many stories are similar to hers, with members enlisting at an early age to begin their service. Since they start so young, most have had significantly greater responsibility at much earlier stages in their careers than their civilian counterparts. They learn team dynamics from the very beginning and function in teams throughout their careers. If one fails, they all fail; if one succeeds, they all succeed. Veterans understand their roles and how their contributions fit with the overall objectives of the team. Outside of athletics at very high levels, there is no better team development incubator than the US military. Even professional athletes understand this; they refer to what they do as "going into battle," "being a warrior on the field," and "giving it their all."

Every role in the military, from top to bottom, has associated metrics that define success. While twenty-two year olds who served four years may not have their college degrees quite yet, they have received very formal education in fields they knew nothing about before they enlisted. While their counterparts enjoyed several spring break trips to exotic vacation destinations, they were deployed multiple times to some of the most dangerous places in the world. While their counterparts balanced twelve-hour credit loads with working ten hours a week as a local barista, veterans balanced a multimillion dollar budget, dozens of personnel, heavy equipment, and numerous assets with a value that cannot be quantified. They do all of this potentially under the risk of great bodily harm or even death in places where they may not be fluent in the native tongue. They are expert decision makers who use the values they have learned to act with integrity and lead by example. They learn and grow by accepting responsibility beyond their traditional jobs and have the ability to be as successful as they would like.

Andrea's final thought is simple yet profound. Military service develops character. Through this character development, it teaches many values,

Strength – The Bond That Holds a Team Together

including discipline, respect, and the importance of accountability. Positional respect is a function of the good order and discipline of the military; individual respect is earned and given in direct proportion to the measure earned. Effective leaders know this and build teams based on mutual respect; their people do not respect them because they have to but because they want to. Andrea has positioned herself well for success beyond military service; she is limited only by the efforts she is willing to put forth to overcome any obstacles in her path.

Corporate Application

How strong is your team, and how do they respond to adversity? Will they stay the course on even the most difficult paths? Do they succeed at all costs but do so within the boundaries of the organization's core values? Do they clearly understand the importance of the team and the role they play not only in their own success but also on the team as a whole? Does your organization value diversity and look to increase it in your workforce? Do you have specific programs in place to increase your pool of highly qualified diverse candidates? If you are looking to recruit candidates with a depth and strength of character that has been tested under some of the most extreme conditions on earth, consider hiring more veterans. If your diverse candidate pool isn't what you would like it to be, consider attracting the best and brightest from the most diverse organization in the world, the US military.

Veteran Application

Which obstacles have you overcome during your military service? Can you clearly define the situation you were in, the actions you took, and the results you achieved? Can you clearly define how you have done this as part of a team and how your actions directly affected the success of the team's mission? How have you operated successfully on diverse teams, and how has the team achieved success in diverse environments around the world? Do you have a clear track record of success against various metrics put in place to measure your results? The more clearly you can define successful results in these areas, the better your chances are of making a smooth transition to employment in the private sector.

Andrea waits at the controls of a Blackhawk before a mission in Iraq.
Photo courtesy of Eric Bowen.

Strength – The Bond That Holds a Team Together

With pre-flight complete, Andrea waits for the final crew briefing before one of many flights in Iraq. Photo courtesy of Eric Bowen.

"Subtlety may deceive you; integrity never will."

- Oliver Cromwell

Chapter 9
Integrity – Black and White or Fifty Shades of Gray?

As we grow older, many of us long for the days when someone's word was their bond and a handshake meant more than any contract one could put in writing and sign. Decisions based on integrity were framed in black and white; the correct path may not have been an easy choice, but it was always the right way, and everyone involved in the situation knew it. Over the years it seems values-based decision making has become far more complicated, as objectively defined values such as integrity have tread a slippery slope where the shade of gray determines a very subjective application of integrity. In other words, integrity is applied differently depending on who is applying it and his or her subjective view of the situation. For Jason Miller, integrity is not a subjective value, and he never has allowed for moral tradeoffs in order to increase his success in any endeavor.

A Major in the US Air Force Reserve, Jason is a veteran with more than ten years of service. He began on active duty after graduating from the University of Iowa on an ROTC scholarship in 2002. He grew up in Iowa, where his mother spent much of his childhood serving the family full time at home before beginning a career in the banking industry. She also balanced family life with pursuing her own education; she earned her associate's degree while her children were still in school, a sacrifice that continues to inspire Jason many years later. His father had a diverse career, beginning in law enforcement and serving in the Army as a Military Policeman. Since leaving the military, his father has primarily focused on project management in the IT world; he also has served in various elected offices in the state of Iowa. Growing up in the heartland, Jason remembers clearly the values his parents instilled in him, which focused on service to others wherever possible. These values have led him to continue a life of service in the Air Force. Beginning in 2002, Jason spent time on active duty at Vandenberg Air Force Base in California and Ramstein Air Base in Germany. In 2010 he transitioned to a reserve slot as a Force Support Officer with the 934th Airlift Wing in Minneapolis. He has deployed twice, both times serving in joint assignments, where he was responsible not just for Air Force personnel but also for support to deployed members from all branches of service. From 2006 to 2007, Jason was assigned to Guantanamo Bay, Cuba, as the Officer in Charge, Joint Personnel Service Center at the Joint Task Force for Detainee Operations. In 2009 he was assigned to the US Embassy in Bogota, Columbia as the Officer in Charge, Joint Personnel Service Center.

Throughout his career, Jason has gone above and beyond whatever was required with the task at hand. He repeatedly has been recognized for his leadership and superior performance both in his job and in the extracurricular activities that helped enrich the lives of his fellow airmen, including involvement in professional organizations such as the Company Grade Officer Council. His leadership and outstanding performance were recognized with his nomination for the Lance P. Sijan USAF Leadership Award and the Company Grade Officer of the Year award, both of which he won at the local level. During his time in the service, he has taken various leadership classes; he completed Squadron Officer School and also was selected for Air Mobility Command's High Flight, a weeklong leadership conference. While serving full time on active duty, Jason worked his way through a management program at the University of Maryland, where he earned his master's degree in 2008. While many people work their way through graduate degree programs, Jason's journey was certainly a challenge. Not only did he have the

INTEGRITY–BLACK AND WHITE OR FIFTY SHADES OF GRAY?

rigors of active duty service, but he also changed duty stations and relocated overseas, deployed to Cuba, and got married. Although it took him several years to complete the program, he toiled relentlessly in an effort to finish what he had started.

For many, service in the military is a calling of sorts. Jason's family fostered this call and built a firm foundation of core values that naturally progressed into his serving his country through military service. Starting from Jason's time in ROTC, the Air Force found a receptive foundation on which to continue to build the structure of values he holds dear. Jason wanted to serve, and he lives a life with no regrets; he did not want to look back and wish he had served when he had the opportunity to do so. As an ROTC student, he began his service prior to 9/11, a time when deployments were minimal and the expected sacrifice was much less. He is one of a new generation of military personnel who enter the service knowing full well the danger that may lie ahead. After 9/11, the easy decision would have been to withdraw from the program and avoid such danger. The world changed forever on 9/11; no one would blame him if he opted for safety instead of facing the risks associated with military service during a time of war. Jason stood firm, however, and this decision shapes his values to this day as he serves without regrets.

While success largely can be measured in direct proportion to the effort a person puts toward his or her success, a portion of success comes as a result of the quality of the mentorship the individual has received. Regardless of the field in which they thrive, humble leaders often credit those who helped guide their development and recognize the important contributions these mentors have made. Jason is no exception; he's had the good fortune of several senior officers having taken an interest in him and providing him with mentorship that altered the course of his career, growing it in ways he could not have foreseen.

One such mentor was a retired Colonel who challenged Jason shortly after he began his time on active duty. As is the case with many new college graduates, the last thing he wanted to do was go back to school after having completed four years of coursework. He never really felt he needed a graduate degree; most of what he needed to know he either learned while obtaining his undergraduate degree or while working on the job; why invest more in a graduate degree? The Colonel disagreed with him, however, and among other things taught him the value of continual self-improvement. He also gave Jason a deeper understanding of what it means to look at the big picture. Jason was correct in his assumption that in the short term he did not need another degree. For the foreseeable future, his career was set. Why worry about additional schooling he may never need or use? Through mentorship from the Colonel and others, however, he came to appreciate the possibility of not simply what is but also what can be. He learned that the value of commitments made today is often not realized until well into the future; much of the time, one does not truly understand the value until additional pieces of the puzzle are obtained and put together. Additionally, Jason developed perseverance by sticking to a path many would have abandoned along the way. Five years is a long time to remain committed to a degree program when you are working full time, new to your job, and fresh out of college. Many of Jason's colleagues were enjoying life and had few cares in the world apart from their day-to-day service in the Air Force. Jason, however, persevered. Today he can look back and see how the bigger picture has developed and the value he now has, having obtained his master's degree in management and transitioning to a career beyond active duty Air Force. Recently he added a project management certification to his credentials and continues to demonstrate his worth in employment apart from the military. He uses his education every day and constantly receives reminders of the value he now derives from the commitment he made long ago. Jason says he is both humble and grateful for the mentorship he has received; he knows unequivocally he would not be the same person he is today without it. In part it helped to transform him into "not your average Joe."

During the course of his career, difficult times have shaped him, beyond the challenges of continuing education and simultaneous service. Perhaps the most difficult of these times was the loss of two friends in separate incidents as a result of combat operations overseas. One was a colleague and the other a close friend and mentor. While those who serve accept the risks associated with military service, it does not make it any easier to deal with

INTEGRITY–BLACK AND WHITE OR FIFTY SHADES OF GRAY?

the loss. Whether deployed or not, even with a loss, Jason had a job to do, and many others counted on him to perform at the highest level he could. With a high operational tempo since 9/11 and precious little downtime, coping with such tragic loss can be extremely difficult. Over time Jason has come to terms with the passing of these friends, even though both died too early and had much more to give to the world. Their deaths undoubtedly have shaped who Jason is today and given him a desire to take up their banner of service to others and continue his own service in honor of their memory and the impact they had in his life.

When I asked Jason what the most meaningful core value is to him, he did not hesitate to say, "Integrity." Part of his definition was similar to many given over the years; doing the right thing when no one is looking. However, he took it a bit further and added a slightly different spin. Integrity to him is doing the right thing regardless of who is looking. He says that it is just as important to do the right thing when someone senior is watching over you as when those junior to you are watching. When he does not know who is watching, be it junior, senior, or someone completely outside of his decision making process, integrity allows him to make decisions consistent with the values he adheres to and never forces him to keep score in an effort to create different versions of the truth depending on who is looking. Many times people change their integrity to match the situation they are in, rather than make decisions based on true integrity. Having served closely with Jason for nearly two years, I can say with complete confidence that he is not one of those people; his integrity always has been above reproach.

Jason offered several personal examples when discussing situations he has experienced that required integrity. One such example was from his time serving on active duty while in Squadron Officer School, known in the Air Force as SOS. It is a leadership course designed to prepare service members for the next steps in their careers and also prepare them to accept a much greater leadership responsibility. As is often the case in the military, the course is team oriented and very competitive. Everything the team does is evaluated and measured; scores are kept, and teams are ranked. As Jason's team, known as a "flight" in the Air Force, neared the end of the course, they were in the running to finish as one of the top flights, an honor all flights strive to earn. One of the few tasks that stood in the way was a timed fitness test. The rankings were close enough that others in the flight felt all their scores need to be above a certain level in order for them to earn flight honors for their performance. Upon completion of the event, there was a single score that was not within the range they needed and ultimately could cost them the honors for which they had worked so hard. Jason was in a position of leadership and responsible for documenting the scores and turning them in. Several others in his flight came to him and asked him to turn numbers in that would ensure their standing as a top flight, but he refused. To him there were no shades of gray; the scores were what they were, and anything reported differently would have been false. Sacrificing his own integrity and that of the entire flight for an honor they would not have fully earned was, in his mind, not the correct choice. Holding firm under the pressure, he turned in the correct scores. Although several members of the flight were angry, he knew he had done the right thing. In the end it turned out they did not need to cheat to win. The scores they had turned in were sufficient to qualify them as a top flight, and they were recognized for their superior performance. Most important, they did it with integrity and honor.

When Jason transitioned from active duty to his current role in the reserves, he also began a career in sales. Here he again found himself in a competitive environment; members of the sales team were competing to bring in the most new prospects. Although he was new to the company, he was doing well, so well that he was tied for first place with the top salesperson in the office. As the contest drew to a close, it was coming down to the wire, with each of them bringing in new prospects. Jason was a rookie in league with an experienced veteran, which did not sit well with the old pro. In an effort to win at all costs and not be shown up by the rookie, the man claimed prospects he had made up, padding his numbers to ensure a victory. Jason could have reacted in many ways, but most of them did not align with his values. He wasn't willing to sacrifice integrity for a victory that ultimately could cost him his job if he cheated. He wasn't willing to perpetuate a culture of deception and dishonesty; if it was happening internally, what was happening to customers being served externally? Jason let the experienced

INTEGRITY—BLACK AND WHITE OR FIFTY SHADES OF GRAY?

salesman know he was aware of the cheating and that it needed to stop. When it didn't stop, he took the only course of action he knew to take and turned him in for falsifying his results. He showed integrity as well as great deal of courage in standing up as the new guy and letting the team know he wouldn't compromise his values. In the end, Jason not only won the contest but also came away from the experience with a much better prize, his integrity intact and respect among some of his peers for having the courage not to maintain the status quo.

Throughout the years, Jason has come to realize one fundamentally important principle as it relates to core values, specifically integrity. No matter the position a person occupies on an organizational chart, from the CEO to the mail clerk and everyone in between, everyone respects integrity. While some organizations struggle with integrity, most people in those companies value integrity in others whether or not they possess it themselves. Why? It's simply because when tough times arise, we all hope those making the decisions have enough integrity to do the right thing, not merely what is convenient and brings about the greatest reward in the short term while completely disregarding the long-term impact.

Think about this for a moment. How many times have you heard a reporter discuss an ethical breach at a company? As more details are revealed, the more sordid the story becomes. Unfortunately these stories are all too common; when employees are asked for their thoughts on situations such as these, they almost always state that a lack of integrity led to the disaster at hand. Conversely, when things are going right, how many employees are disgruntled and wish leadership would have *less* integrity when making critical decisions? Have you ever heard employees question a business decision by stating they don't understand why the company's leadership has so much integrity? Of course not; integrity is a valuable commodity, one that should be applied evenly and consistently and never based on the various shades of gray many will see in a given situation. When individuals serve with integrity, those above and below them in the organization never will be able to call their character into question. Those below know they will make the right decision for the team and not seek to fulfill their own self-interests.

Those above trust them with the reputation of the organization and know they can count on them to make complex decisions that will lend further credibility to the team's reputation.

As my interview with Jason came to an end, he had a few final thoughts to share with veterans looking to improve their worth in the job market and with employers considering making proactive efforts to hire more veterans. First and foremost, Jason says, today's veterans all serve voluntarily. They stepped forward to answer their nation's call to serve in order to protect the freedoms we cherish. As a result it is fair to say they are dedicated; it is why they joined in the first place, to serve a cause greater than themselves. They have passion and an inner drive to succeed. In many cases, if they did not incorporate these qualities in the roles they performed, the risk of injury or death would increase exponentially. Attempting to achieve success on any mission can spark very high levels of stress. Success comes only for those who can remain effective no matter the stress associated with any situation they face.

When compared to their civilian counterparts, veterans often have received the opportunity to take on roles that required adapting, changing, or adding skills in order to achieve success. Traditionally, they receive far more responsibility much earlier in their careers, and their success is tied directly not only to their own efforts but also the effectiveness of their leadership and the impact it has on the team's performance. Military service builds and develops leadership skills early and often. This experience typically cannot be obtained anywhere else. Hiring veterans not only feels good; it simply makes good business sense.

Corporate Application

Does your organization display integrity in all it does, or is integrity inconsistently applied based on the situation at hand? Integrity is a value that must be driven from the top down. If leadership has no integrity, the resulting cultural norm will directly reflect the commonly accepted values of those in charge. If your staff's integrity is a direct reflection of who you are as a leader, would you trust everyone on your team to always make the right

Integrity–Black and White or Fifty Shades of Gray?

decision based on the values they have and the values you have displayed for them? If not, why? Integrity is not accidental; it is intentional. How are you building it throughout your organization? Could hiring veterans help you build a deeper culture of integrity?

Veteran Application

What does integrity mean to you as a veteran? Are you able to clearly define this during an interview with a potential employer? Can you clearly discuss specific examples of how you have applied integrity in your decision making processes? Has your integrity ever been called into question? If so, what did you do to resolve the situation? Have you ever failed to have integrity when you should have? Which specific actions did you take to resolve the situation, and what did you learn that provides additional value to an employer who may face a similar situation with his or her employees?

If the assumption is correct that integrity is a value employers always need and one you possess with clearly defined examples of how you have lived it, are you sharing this during interviews to demonstrate the value you bring? Always sell yourself and the skills you have that are directly applicable to the position for which you are interviewing. You should never, however, sell your experience based solely on your skills at the expense of the core values you bring to any employment opportunity, especially when it comes to integrity.

Jason meeting the Commander in Chief during a base visit

Jason receiving a Meritorious Service Medal

Chapter 10
Why Hire Joe?
Values Versus Skills Based Hiring

Without question, most veterans bring a wealth of experience and vast responsibility that outpaces those of their counterparts in the private sector. They have operated in diverse environments around the world under some of the most dangerous and austere conditions imaginable. They are adept at working with many technology platforms and possess the cognitive aptitude to learn and become proficient in nearly any job in short order.

Most of all, veterans bring values that have been forged in the crucible of military service. A blacksmith forges a sword in much the same way that the military forges values. The blacksmith takes raw material and applies massive heat, changing it from a solid to a more malleable form. He then takes various tools of his trade, such as a hammer and anvil, to shape his sword through the application of repeated blunt force. If necessary, he heats the metal again so he can continue to apply the force needed to produce both a weapon of war and a work of art. Once the blacksmith is satisfied with the shape, the metal goes through a tempering process in which alternating heat and cold are applied in order to maximize its strength and durability. Once the metal is tempered, the blacksmith sharpens the edge by applying progressively finer abrasives at precisely the right angles to obtain maximum sharpness. Finally, the blacksmith finishes the sword by adding final details and polishing the surface for all to admire. Two things are clear during this process; first, when beginning with raw materials, one cannot make a sword without applying heat, pressure, tremendous force, stress, and abrasives. Second, while the sword is most recognized as a weapon of war, it is also a beautiful piece of art that is forged through strictly observed methods to achieve the desired beauty. If the viewer simply focuses on the sword being a weapon of war, he or she will miss the true value the sword brings to the world.

Such is the case with the value of the veteran in employment beyond the military. Similar to the sword, veterans begin their journeys as raw material. They are forged with heat, pressure, tremendous force, stress, and abrasives that shape and mold them into finished products. While they are clearly capable of being weapons of war, this is not their defining characteristic, and most are never used in this fashion. Almost all veterans come through the refining process to become a work of art. The forging process is lengthy and continues long after the initial process is complete; it must continue lest the sword lose its edge.

So how is this analogy applicable to hiring veterans? To properly answer this question, you must first understand your company's current culture. Does your organization hire new employees whose values have been forged in a fashion similar to that of the sword? If not, do you have a foundry on site to begin the forging process with new employees to build the values that will fit best into your organizational culture? If this is not standard practice, does your organization merely trust that the values are present and were forged properly before a potential new employee even reaches you?

Why Hire Joe? Values Versus Skills Based Hiring

While most employers want to hire individuals with values that match those of their organization, the most common hiring model focuses almost exclusively on skills. The reasons for this are many but include the following: those in the hiring process are doing more with less and need to hire candidates who appear to have exactly the skills needed to do the job; the use of technology in the hiring process focuses almost exclusively on filtering out those who are not a skills or keyword match; and most involved in the hiring process are inexperienced and/or not highly skilled when it comes to interviewing techniques that will determine the true worth of a candidate. The focus is predominantly on skills instead of values, as it is most often easiest to quantify or measure skills and move toward a hire as quickly as possible. Figure 1 below graphically illustrates the skills based hiring model.

SKILLS BASED HIRING

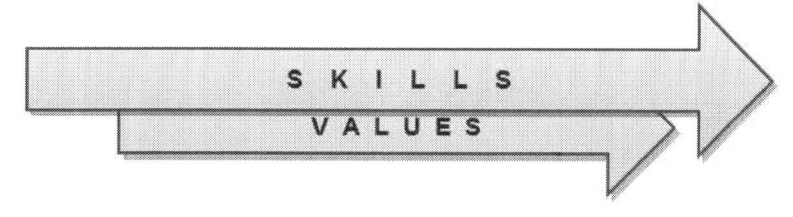

Figure 1

As illustrated in Figure 1, hiring typically is based first on a skills match and an assumption that when the skills match the position, the values should underlie the skills. While this may be the case, the relationship is not one of causation but rather correlation at best, meaning values may or may not be present when one hires solely based on skills. A more accurate model is needed—one that captures both skills and values while illustrating the relationship between the two.

VALUES vs SKILLS HIRING

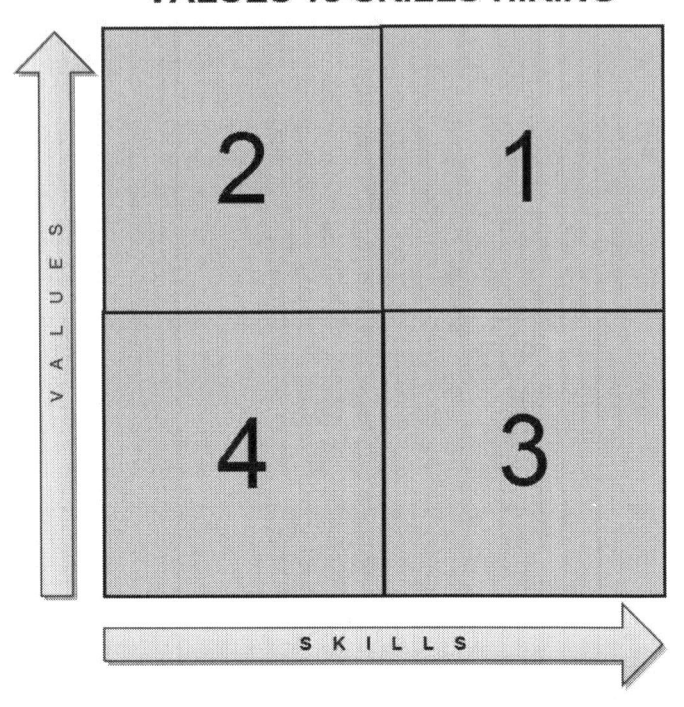

	2	1
	4	3

VALUES ↑

SKILLS →

Figure 2

As illustrated in Figure 2, skills and values operate independently of each other. It is possible to hire a candidate with low skills/low values, high skills/low values, high values/low skills, or high values/high skills. If it can be avoided, no company seeks to hire those occupying block 4. The ideal hire for most companies would be those in block 1. Many companies, however, use the hiring model in Figure 1. They assume values are present and that they are hiring in block 1, but in reality the values do not meet expectations and they hire from block 3. Hiring based on skills while assuming values are present can have devastating implications for any organization. When values are not present in a workforce, the organization may not have the time or ability to build them, and inevitably employee-relations issues will develop, which can affect productivity, customer relations, morale, employee retention, and much more.

Why Hire Joe? Values Versus Skills Based Hiring

VALUES vs SKILLS HIRING

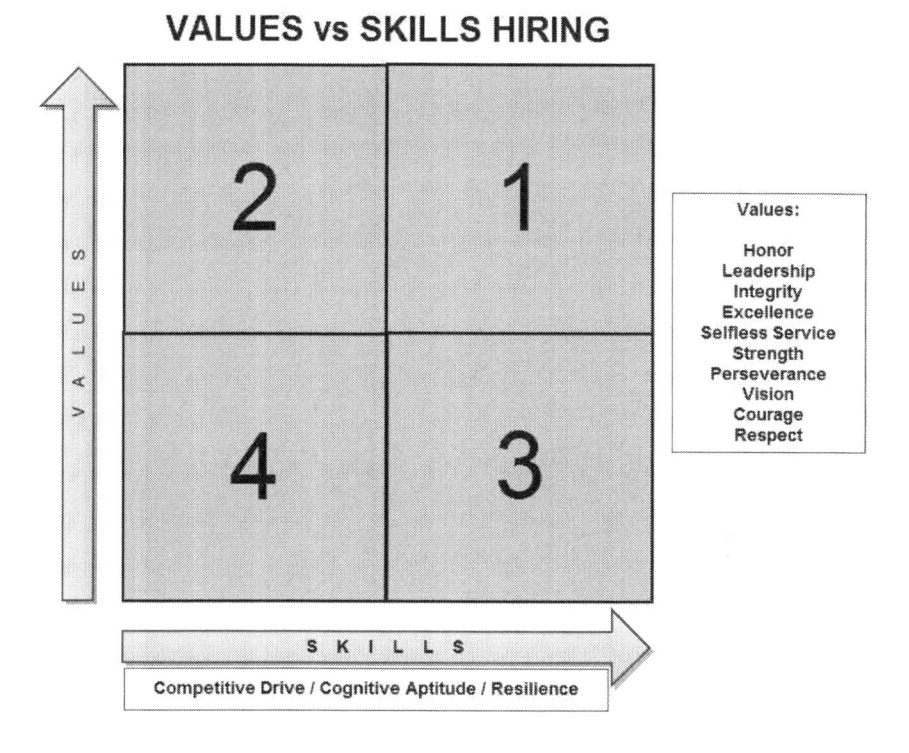

[Figure: A 2x2 matrix with VALUES on the vertical axis and SKILLS on the horizontal axis. The quadrants are numbered 2 (top-left), 1 (top-right), 4 (bottom-left), and 3 (bottom-right). The SKILLS axis is labeled "Competitive Drive / Cognitive Aptitude / Resilience". A side box lists Values: Honor, Leadership, Integrity, Excellence, Selfless Service, Strength, Perseverance, Vision, Courage, Respect.]

Figure 3

Figure 3 illustrates a balanced approach that uses a values hiring matrix, rather than one that is skills based. Hiring decisions should be made primarily in blocks 2 and 1, in which potential employees have strong values and display a minimum base of skills that can be expanded upon in short order. Not only is the focus on hiring first for values, but it also shifts the skills needed for the position to a broad base of skills that are universally applicable in most positions. Competencies such as competitive drive, cognitive aptitude, and resilience are skills an employer can build upon and refine with more specific skills directly applicable to the position being filled. Simply put, hiring candidates with the right values and a good base of skills that can be further developed is good business sense.

As demonstrated throughout *Not Your Average Joe*, veterans reside firmly in blocks 2 and 1 in the hiring matrix in Figure 3. They have values forged in the same manner as a beautifully crafted sword as well as the ability to quickly adapt to almost any environment while gaining the skills needed to perform at or above expectations. Veterans have served in positions of great responsibility and are capable of adding tremendous value beyond their military service. Employers who understand the value of veterans and the return on investment that comes with hiring the right veterans have a distinctive competitive advantage in the market in terms of hiring and retaining the best employees. If you're looking to hire the best or create sustainable internal veteran hiring initiatives at your company, consider turning to the best.

Metafrazo, LLC, provides strategic consulting resources to develop or improve existing talent acquisition practices of veterans in companies of all sizes. Services include the creation of strategic plans to identify, attract, and hire the right veterans in roles that will position both the company and veterans for the greatest success. Additionally, the firm offers consulting services in regard to veteran development, promotion, and retention programs.

For more information visit www.metafrazo.net

www.facebook.com/metafrazo
www.twitter.com/metafrazo
www.linkedin.com/company/2437692?trk=tyah

Honoring those who have served

United States Army

Victor Ames, *Homer C. Anderson*, Jason P. Anderson, Roy Otto Anderson, Bruce Banta, Sarah Banta, Eric Berens, Andrea Bond, Harry Bras, *L.W. "Joe" Brandes*, Chad Byers, *Felipe Cases*, *James A. Cochran*, Ted Daley, Aaron Davis, David Denton, Bob Dettmer, Jennifer Diaz, Alan Duff, Giacomo DiGiacomo, Sarah A. Washington Ephraim, Scott Garrison, *Michael Girdano*, *Lodwyck Hardenbrook*, William Hecker III, Ed Herman, Charles Hollenback, Robert Hosman, Rob Jackson, *William H. "Buckwheat" Jenkins*, Bruce Jensen, *Clyde Alfred (Jack) Knapp*, David Knapp, Scott Koscielniak, Victor Krull, Jerry Kyser, Brett Larson, Richard Leonard, Michael D. Lewis, Adam McDowell, Andrew McLean, Jacob McLellan, Micah McLellan, Scott McLellan, Joel Miller, *Hector D. Montero*, Rene Montero, *Axel Hilmer Nelson*, *Donald R. Nordblom*, Jeff Pratt, Joe Roushar, Terry "T" Stade, Kent Teeter, *Wiltse Lee Weber*

Not Your Average Joe

United States Navy

Craig Benson, Margie Binder, Anthony Bohaty, Cameron Byers, Duncan Byers, David J. Cochran, David M. Cochran, Thomas Cooper, Philip Dana, Roger Davis, Christian Fager, Arthur Eugene Kihlstadius, Dennis Kihlstadius, Thomas Kihlstadius, Jack Knapp, William A. Martin, Nicholas Mullen, Robert P. Nelson, *Jackie L. Nordblom, Dean J. Smith, Ron Vauk*, Keith Wettschreck

★

United States Marine Corps

Kevin Bridges, Chad Brooks, Michael Cannell, Wayne Cannell, Jesse Gerhard, *Raymond John Hagberg*, Larry Kihlstadius, Patrick Logan, Allen Mostue, Roy H. Nordblom III, Alex Plechash, Tim Simmons, Shawn Whitney

★

United States Coast Guard

George Heller

★

United States Air Force

Chris Berens, Scott Braski, Donald Byers, Corey Murray Davis, Dennis Davis, Matt Collins, Nathanial George, Steve Gray, Dick Hanson, Dave Hardy, Alvin E. Hopson III, Joy C. Hopson, Jeff Imsdahl, Matt Johnson, Carlton Lebroke, Diana Liedtke-Thorpe, Kristen Maloney, Roy Edward Menne, Jason Miller, Roy H. Nordblom, Jr, Bob Nunnally, Joe Rodwell, Bill Teague, *John Worley*

Names in italics recognized posthumously

Many Thanks To Our Sponsorship Partners
They Are Anything But Average Joes!

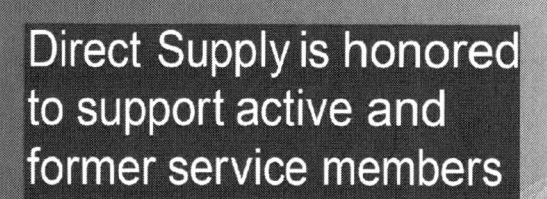

Direct Supply is honored to support active and former service members

Our thriving community of men and women in uniform is a critical component of our diverse company culture. These individuals apply valuable skill sets to help us achieve our mission – to enhance the lives of America's seniors. As the nation's leading supplier of equipment, eCommerce and service solutions to the Senior Living industry, we're proud to employ America's dedicated veterans.

➤ Major Jason Miller serves in the U.S. Air Force Reserve. Direct Supply is fortunate to have him apply his talents as a Senior Operations Manager.

DIRECT SUPPLY®

Visit directsupply.com/careers to learn more today.

© 2013 Direct Supply, Inc. All rights reserved.

EVER-GREEN ENERGY™

Ever-Green Energy employees are key to our success and we value their unique contributions. Our employees showcase experience in industrial operations and development, energy generation and distribution, construction, engineering, non-profit and for-profit accounting and finance, information technology and utility metering, human resources, communications, and energy education. Ever-Green continues to develop a diverse and complex talent base for our growing organization and would not be a recognized industry leader without the skills and experience of our multi-faceted team.

ADVANCING WITH HONOR

Life Technologies is a global biotechnology company that is committed to providing the most innovative products and services to leading customers in the fields of scientific research, genetic analysis and applied sciences. Life Technologies has approximately 10,000 employees and had sales of $3.8 billion in 2012.

We're hiring

Contact Philip Dana
Senior Manager, Talent Acquisition
(ex-Navy & Naval Academy graduate)

- linkedin.com/in/militarytalent
- twitter.com/militarytalent
- pinterest.com/militarytalent

life technologies

ONLINE TRADING ACADEMY

Words cannot express our gratitude for the service of all current members and veterans of the US military. Your integrity, dedication and loyalty provide us tremendous freedom. It is your selfless sacrifice which provides an example for all to follow.

Thank You & May

God bless you.

At OTA we offer professional instruction in state-of-the-art teaching facilities around the world and a wide array of home study materials. We have a community of over 30,000 students that have learned to trade with the skill and confidence of professional traders. You have served us, how may we serve you?

Online Trading Academy of MN
www.otaminn.com
(952) 814-4410

BFW CHARITIES

Veteran Pain Program

Nearly 400,000 veterans in MN • 80,000 or more may be experiencing service-connected disabilities due to musculoskeletal conditions. • Total cost of veteran service-connected compensation reaches an estimated $36.5 billion each year.

952-893-8900 • www.BFWCharities.com

"As a veteran who has experienced chronic back pain for nearly 20 years, finding the pain clinic was a true blessing. I no longer experience the back pain, I am sleeping better than I have in years and my overall health is excellent. Best of all, I have not paid a single penny for it. I beleive in what they are doing and you should too."
-Dennis Davis, Author of *Not Your Average Joe*

Join Our Cause

We believe that our veterans can make a complete recovery with the support and resources provided by BFW Charities and its community partners working together.

See how you can get involved at
www.BFWCharities.com

Made in the USA
Charleston, SC
04 June 2013